MURI
— and —
MAYHEM
— in the —
WEST!

Veronica Smith

REDCLIFFE
Bristol

First published in 1993 by
Redcliffe Press Ltd
49 Park St, Bristol.

© *Veronica Smith*

ISBN 1 872971 43 1

British Cataloguing-in-Publication Data.
A catalogue record for this book is available
from the British Library.

Typeset and printed by
The Longdunn Press Ltd., Bristol.

Contents

Introduction

It took very little persuasion for me to embark on this, my second book of local murders. I even received requests for the inclusion of certain 'favourite' crimes – so Auntie Elsie (Ellery), Doreen Jackson and Jack Andrews, I am sorry to disappoint you but we felt the Cornock case too sensitive a subject for inclusion. Great care has been taken on all subject matter in this book so as not to cause distress or offence to any members of families concerned with the crimes. Reference to any living person has been made with their full consent.

During the course of my research different crime patterns emerged which interested me. The late 'forties and early 'fifties seem to have produced robbery-related killings which may have reflected the American gangster films so popular in this era. Roman Redel ('The Bank Bandits who Boarded a Bus') married a cinema usherette. Could he have been influenced by the Saturday night 'flick at the Metropole?

During these early post-war years my family lived next door to Dt. Inspector Jesse Pane and his smashing wife Dorrie who was my mother's best friend. Although never a word was leaked from number 13 about these cases I felt as if I was caught up in the drama of it all, albeit on the fringe, as I sat on their doorstep swapping comics with their son, Anthony.

I particularly enjoyed working on the rural tales. Just reading those old newspaper reports of tavern-talk and events like the Longney Feast transported me back in time. I pondered the difference between today's killers and those of long ago. The motives were the same – lust, greed, jealousy – so what had changed? As I read the confessions of those about to take that last short walk to eternity it occurred to me how strong the power of religion was in those days. The convicted were forced to face the terrible wrong they had done and make their peace with their Maker. Perhaps the prospect of certain death at a specified time on a designated day brings an overwhelming longing for the comfort of a religion which has been pushed aside for many a long year. Confessions were published in full detail and always ended with exhortations never to follow the path to Hell that the prisoners had trod. Propaganda? Perhaps. It did seem to act as a deterrent though, did it not?

The important part played by the Local Studies staff in various libraries throughout the West of England cannot be overestimated. They have all taken such trouble to provide me with the information I needed. Helen Wright at Gloucester even popped out in her lunch hour to check on an architectural detail for me. So thank you, Helen, also Mrs Turton at Gloucester, Shirley Wickham at Dorchester, Linda Matthews and Wendy Bates at Trowbridge and J.R. Elliot and staff at Plymouth; also Sue Sloman, Bath Art Gallery and Mrs E. Bevan, Bath Library.

I should also like to express my appreciation, once again, to Bristol Central Library staff and Gerry Brooke, Bristol Evening Post, for letting me loose amongst his files.

My thanks to my uncle, Lionel Ellery, for help on geographical details of Plymouth, to Joe Mawson for setting me on the Trowbridge trail, to Sue Lee for combing the countryside with me and Hayley Goodwin for high-speed typing to help me meet my deadline.

Apologies to my stepmother, Poppy Peck, whom I have neglected recently in favour of box-loads of old newspaper cuttings.

Special thanks, too, to John, Angela and Clara Sansom whom I have come to regard as friends rather than just publishers.

I SHOULD LIKE TO DEDICATE THIS BOOK TO MY DAUGHTER, MANDIE BRITTON, AND TO THE STAFF AND DOCTORS OF THE INTENSIVE CARE UNIT AND WARD 5, BRISTOL ROYAL IN-FIRMRY WHO SAVED HER LIFE AFTER A NEAR-FATAL ROAD ACCIDENT IN MARCH 1993.

Steadman's Soothing Strychnine

In spite of Edwin Bailey's illegitimacy he had a better start in life than many children in his position in early Victorian England. He was born in Winterbourne which then, together with neighbouring Frampton Cotterell, was the hub of a thriving hat industry. Vaughn's and Christie's were the two major manufacturers and Edwin's young mother, herself the daughter of a hat maker, worked at Vaughn's. The father, a hat-clipper, either could not or would not marry her and Edwin was brought up in his grandparents' home. He was educated at Winterbourne National School and, on reaching the age of 16, was placed by his uncle as an apprentice with Mr Parry, a bootmaker, in Downend, Bristol. Within a week he was home again following a serious complaint lodged by his employer's wife, regarding his behaviour. In the light of his later conduct we can only suppose he made a pass at her.

What became of him in the next few years is not known but in the early 1860s he started working for Mr Massingham who ran a shoe shop in Mary-le-Port Street. His uncle eventually bought the business and appointed Edwin manager. His mother, meanwhile, had at last achieved respectability by virtue of marriage to a man who worked in a local sugar refinery and she had set up home in Bristol.

Edwin was lodging in Stapleton Road, Easton. After quarrelling with his uncle and finding himself jobless he married his landlady, an older woman of means. Using his newly-acquired fortune he persuaded a young man of his acquaintance to go into the wholesale business with him. The venture failed, Edwin was bankrupted and his partner left destitute. The financial ruin caused the breakdown of the young partner's health and he died soon afterwards. His embittered widow attempted to warn Bailey's next landlord of his untrustworthiness but her cautions were ignored. The premises on St Augustine's Parade mysteriously caught fire but were fortunately saved, thus wrecking Edwin's insurance claim hopes. After this fiasco he disappeared to London for a year and worked in a friend's tavern there.

Edwin returned to Bristol and his patient wife for a while, then took off again – this time to Gloucester. He worked at Jacobs boot shop and, posing as a single man, started courting one of his fellow assistants. During his stay in Gloucester he became involved with a group of Atheists. He also ran up debts at various shops. The object of his attentions turned out to be a policeman's daughter and some of his colleagues had knowledge of Edwin, including the fact that he had a wife in Bristol. To save the girl's honour, they had Edwin run out of town.

Back came Edwin to Bristol where he resumed work in the boot business, this time setting up his own place in Boyce's Avenue, Clifton, a venture probably financed by his wife. It was at around this time he met Anne Barry who lived in St James Barton above a china shop. Whether or not she was actually married to Louis Barry, a North American army veteran, is open to speculation. It was said her real name was Salmond. Louis worked as a porter, she as a midwife among the poor of the area. She supplemented her income by charring and one of the shops she cleaned was that belonging to Edwin Bailey. It's not clear just what their relationship was, but he did visit her often in the Barton and sent postcards to her. She was a small, slim, pale woman with glittering dark eyes and she certainly seemed to be in thrall to the womanizing bootmaker.

In 1871 a young servant by the name of Mary Susan Jenkins was sent by her master to Edwin's shop to have some boots repaired. According to Mary, Edwin seized her and dragged her into the back of the shop where he gagged her before raping her. She reported him to the police saying he used 'great violence' on her.

Just how he managed to assault her again in February 1872 is never explained. On this occasion he made her pregnant and on October 23rd, 1872 she gave birth to a daughter whom she named Sarah.

Though he stoutly denied he was the father of Mary's child the Magistrate decided otherwise and he was ordered to pay five shillings a week until the child reached the age of 16. It was alleged he was already making payments for another daughter, the mother of whom lived in the Easton area.

Elizabeth and James Jenkins, Mary's parents, seemed to have accepted the situation and made a home for Mary and her baby at Myrtle Cottage described as being 'In Horfield in the Parish of Stapleton'.

By Christmas 1872 Mary, now 18, had managed to find herself a position in Cheltenham Road and her mother agreed to look after the baby. Everyone was very fond of little Sarah and, while she may not have been blessed with material wealth, she was much loved.

It was at about this time that Anne Barry entered their lives. Just how she managed to engineer a meeting with the family one can only speculate but she was soon visiting on a regular basis. She said the child reminded her of her own baby whom she had 'buried at Brighton,' and she brought Sarah presents including a dress she had fashioned, she said, for her own sister's child which had sadly died. When Mary was offered the job in Cheltenham Road Anne offered to look after the baby but was told firmly that arrangements had already been made.

The Jenkins' benefactress never told them her surname and sometimes said she lived in Kingsdown, sometimes in St James Barton. She said her husband was called Louis and he was working in a low-paid job in Broad Street 'to get his character back', i.e. to obtain references as he had obviously been in trouble of some sort, even prison. She encouraged Mary and her mother to talk about Sarah's father and was told he lived in Boyce's Avenue. Anne said she did not know that part of Clifton at all. Whenever reference was made to the errant father she would always make some comment like 'Blackguard'.

As the year wore on Mrs Barry began to talk of a charitable institution known as 'The Dorcas Society' and she told the Jenkins' that someone would be contacting them before long. Sure enough on August 13th a letter arrived from a 'Jane Isabella Smith' of Hope Cottages, Cotham. She sent some 'Steadman's Soothing Powders' for the child who had been suffering from teething and digestive problems. She promised she would be sending some clothes for the baby within the next few days.

The following day Anne Barry made one of her visits and was told about the gift. She said she strongly recommended 'Steadman's powders' and would use them in preference to the magnesium mixture the Jenkins favoured. As she took her leave of them she said she would not be calling again as she was 'going to remove to a distant part of Bristol'.

Elizabeth and Mary wrote a letter of thanks to Miss Smith and a day or so later Mary, at home on a day off from her new situation in Berkeley Road, Horfield, decided to administer some of the powder to little Sarah who was suffering from swollen gums. She mixed one of the powders with Sarah's food but as soon as the little mite had swallowed some of the mixture she began to scream. Mary took her into the garden to try to calm her down but to no avail. Elizabeth came out to see what was going on as the child screeched even louder. They thought perhaps a pin had stuck in her but could find none. Meanwhile the child was clenching its fists, throwing its head back as its body was becoming stiff and rigid and its face was turning black. Mary ran off to fetch a doctor but by the time she returned her little Sarah was dead. The remaining powders were analysed by the police and found to contain rat poison which had a strychnine base. Sarah had been murdered.

The letter the two women had sent to Jane Isabella Smith ended up in the Post Office's Dead Letter department. There was no such person, no such address. The police made enquiries and naturally their suspicions fell at once on the reluctant father, Edwin Bailey. They examined papers at his shop comparing his handwriting to that on the letter from Miss Smith. It seemed it was penned by the same hand although efforts had been made to make the Smith letter appear to have been written by a woman. It was thought Bailey had fled the country but he returned to the city before long and was arrested at once. Soon afterwards Anne Barry was also taken into custody. She swore she was innocent of anything other than infiltrating the Jenkins household to try to discover the true identity of Sarah's father as Bailey was totally convinced the child was not his. He held to this belief to his dying moments; whatever else he admitted he always denied he was the father of Mary's child.

Bailey was charged with wilful murder and Anne Barry with aiding and abetting – both were to end their lives on the gallows for this crime. Anne's loyalty to Bailey, who remained completely impassive throughout the court proceedings, was remarkable. Had he paid a high price for her silence? Even had he done so this could not have been the whole story. The philandering bootmaker must have been possessed of an amazingly charismatic personality. Anne professed to love her husband deeply, as she may well have done, but Bailey seems to have had a strange hold over her as he did over his oft-betrayed wife. He wrote his wife a touching letter just before he went to his death and she and others of his family came to visit him during his last few days in prison. He also wrote a farewell letter and poem to 'Miss M'. Could she have been the girl from Easton, mother of his acknowledged daughter?

The day of execution finally dawned. January 12th, 1874. They shared the day with Edward Butt, the Arlingham murderer. As Anne Barry faced her final drop into eternity she instinctively reached out to touch Edwin's hand but because of the strapping around her binding her arms she could not reach. She must have felt very much alone, her husband being incarcerated in Chichester prison at the time on a felonius charge. She had requested that she be hanged in a black silk dress but this was refused so she walked to the scaffold in a pale print calico gown. She expressed great concern as to what would become of her husband once she was dead. She feared, she said, he would 'return to his old ways.'

Both made a full confession of their guilt before they met their Maker and vowed that they truly repented. Just before she died, Anne whispered to the hangman 'This is just what my dream told me I would come to.' Of the three of them Anne took the longest to die.

Murder in Marlborough Buildings

'A dreadful crime has been perpetrated in Bath,' announced the local press on February 4th, 1828.

The victim was 25-year-old Maria Bagnall, a rather superior lady's maid in the employ of Mrs Coxe of East Burnham near Maidenhead who was 'presently residing at number 16 Marlborough Buildings, Bath'.

The alarm was raised at two o'clock on the morning of January 26th. The watchman was alerted to trouble when two shots were fired in the house, one at the front and one at the back and he sounded his rattle to summon assistance while he entered the premises. The butler, Richard Gillham had fired the shots as he had heard suspicious sounds and then found the door at the foot of the garrett stairs leading to the room where he slept with his wife, had been barred. As the watchman was going to his assistance Gillham forced the offending door open. It was discovered the back door

Marlborough Buildings, Bath.

to the property was unlocked, the garden gate unsecured and it seemed as if the intruders had made their escape from the rear of the house.

They then went below to the kitchen and Maria was found near the fireplace lying face downwards, her frilled cap a few feet away from her. A bludgeon lay beside her and her throat had been gashed so deeply that the windpipe and arteries were divided. Her left hand was bruised and the third finger on her right hand almost completely severed.

Mr King, a surgeon from Brook Street, arrived to examine the body at about half past two and formed the conclusion that the girl had been dead between two and three hours. The house was then searched and the ground floor rooms were found to be in total disorder with all the drawers and cupboards ransacked. A silver tea urn lay on the stairs.

On the drawing room table stood four bottles which had contained port, sherry, calcavella and gin. The bottles had been virtually emptied by whoever had committed the crime.

The Corporation of Bath and the Parish Officers offered a reward of £150 between them in an attempt to track down whoever had carried out the awful deed.

Before many days had elapsed Gillham came under suspicion by virtue of blood stains being found on his waistcoat and breeches. The explanation for this was simple, he said. When he had entered the kitchen with the watchman he 'took hold of the body, to raise it.' He was asked whether he had any property apart from that at Marlborough Buildings and he replied in the negative.

Shortly afterwards it was discovered that Gillham had stored a quantity of goods at the house of one, Roberts, an ostler, who lived at number 6 Williams Place, at the back of Northampton Street. These items were taken to the Guildhall and Gillham was interrogated once more. Again he made his denials but on the following day, Thursday, the goods in question were placed in such a position that his glance would fall on them immediately he entered the room. At first when this happened he betrayed little emotion. The articles displayed were contained in 'three hampers, three boxes, a frail basket and a saucepan'. There was a miscellany of knives, forks, fire irons, wine, china, candlesticks and tin ware. Mrs Coxe had identified all of the items as her property. Richard Gillham was asked how he came by these things, although the Mayor did advise him not to answer if he felt reluctant to do so. An early version of reading the prisoner his rights, it would appear.

Gillham was becoming more and more uneasy by the hour and on Friday Mr Bourne, the gaoler, suggested to him that he might like to consult a spiritual adviser. Gillham readily assented and the chaplain, Reverend Marshall visited him at eleven in the morning and spent two hours with him. He returned at three that afternoon and as a result Gillham made a full confession to Mr Bourne.

He stated that he and his pregnant wife had gone up to bed at about eleven o'clock. They had passed Maria on the way and had bid her goodnight. As they were preparing to get into bed Gillham told his wife that he had to go down again as 'his bowels were disordered'. He descended the stairs and took a stick from his pantry, 'one which I had cut some months since'. Apparently Maria was in the habit of going into the kitchen to wash her feet after everyone else had retired for the night and it was so this night. Gillham encountered her by the kitchen door and beat her about the head until she sank to the floor. He continued to rain blows on her as she lay there screaming that she would have him hanged. As she continued to yell he knelt on her, took his pocket knife from his waistcoat pocket and slit her throat. Gillham then calmly dusted himself down, returned the knife to his pocket to be washed and replaced in the table drawer in his room the next day. He then had to make it appear as though burglars had slain her as she had surprised them in their lawless act. He stole a few halfpennies from Maria's purse, washed his hands and went back up to the garrett where his wife was dozing. 'What is the matter?' she asked sleepily. He warned her to 'say nothing about it to the old woman, Nanny.' In fact, he instructed her to say nothing about him going downstairs to anyone but was to say that he had gone to bed before her were she asked.

Gillham returned downstairs, placing the tea urn strategically on the stairs to make it seem that the burglars had dropped it in their flight. He had already disordered the rooms and thrown away some of the liquor. He placed the bludgeon beside the maid's body. The actual weapon he burned the following morning. He swore he had no accomplice and that his wife was completely ignorant of the whole sordid affair.

The curious fact that the whole operation was carried out without anyone hearing sound is explained by the geography of the house. At the very top in the garrett Richard and his wife slept and the old housemaid Anne Spackman (Nanny) also had her room at the other end of the garrett. The old lady was very deaf. Mrs Coxe and Maria had their quarters on the floor below, in the large attic. It would seem reasonable to suppose that Mrs Coxe herself was not at home on the fatal night.

Gillham's savage attack on Maria was motivated by revenge. He had overheard her speak unfavourably of him to their employer. He was, in fact, under notice to quit when the deed was committed and considered Maria to blame for this.

When Gillham was taken back to the prison for the next interrogation at the Guildhall he had to be protected from the incensed mob who were after his blood. The following Sunday he was transported to Shepton Mallet for trial. His execution was not carried out until the following June for reasons that are not entirely clear but may have been partly out of consideration for his unfortunate wife who gave birth at the end of May. He always protested that she was wholly innocent of any involvement. She was very bitter towards him when she discovered what he had done.

Richard Gillham was 25 years old when he committed the monstrous murder. He must have been a pretty cool character to plan the crime and execute it with such efficiency. A local sculptor,

Mr L. Galhagan who operated from number 4 Lower Walks, Bath, made an impression of both murderer and victim but I can find no evidence to suggest these ghoulish relics have survived.

Mrs Coxe had Maria buried in Walcot churchyard and paid to have a stone erected in her memory. Anne Spackman was also interred there when she died, aged 76, the following year.

Before he died Richard Gillham penned the following verse to his former employer:

> From the lone corners of a dreary cell
> To you my Mistress I the truth will tell
> Not in the hope that you will interfere
> To save a life to me no longer dear
>
> Once in my soul reign'd innocence and truth,
> To vice a stranger in the days of youth,
> To you I came, my character unstain'd,
> And with that character I long remain'd,
>
> Bnt yet unknown, your confidence betray'd
> And made my victim, your poor helpless maid,
> More honest far than I true to her trust,
> In manners kind, in every matter just.
>
> I envied her, her justly well- earn'd fame,
> And robb'd at once of being and a name.
> Faithless to you, while cruel and unkind,
> The thought most deeply harrows up my mind.
>
> No longer here her pardon I can crave,
> Untimely sent, to an untimely grave,
> And that by me! that is my time to live,
> Tho' she cannot may God and you forgive,
>
> Great are my sufferings, greater far my crime,
> Happy the man who warning take in time.

Bloodshed at Lloyds Bank

It was mid-afternoon on a chilly January day in 1949 when Mrs Audrey Ball crossed over to the corner of Broad Walk, Bristol to meet her neighbour, Mrs Davies. The doors of the bank which stood on that corner were open and she heard a crash inside. Almost immediately a man who looked pale and appeared to be rather shaken left the bank, closing the door behind him. He was clad in a dark overcoat and hat and carried a brief case. He muttered something to himself as he climbed into an Austin Saloon and pulled away.

A man then emerged from a nearby telephone kiosk and ran across the road. He leapt on to the running board of the Austin and was punched in the face by the driver, who then accelerated causing the partly open door to swing towards the injured man, striking his head.

In a short space of time the whole area was swarming with police. The crash heard by the two women had been the report of a gun – George Black the 50-year-old bank manager had been shot dead and his attacker had fled with £1,430 in £5, £1 and ten shilling notes.

Gradually a picture of the afternoon's events was assimilated. The bank on that busy Friday afternoon was staffed by George Black and his cashier, Donald Twitt, aged 17. At two o'clock a youngish man, bespectacled and respectably dressed entered the bank and explained to Mr Black that he was waiting for a man called Murray, a bookmaker. He spent most of that afternoon in the bank, leaving briefly at one point and, on returning, took a seat at one of the tables. As he sat there local business people came in to bank their takings including John Rowe, a trainer at the Knowle greyhound stadium. A couple of the customers asked the man if he was waiting to be served but both received a negative reply and the explanation that he was waiting for someone.

A local vicar, the Rev. Johnson of St Barnabas in Daventry Road got a good look at the man who, as the vicar left the bank, was penning a note to Murray which read:

See you Monday.
Missed you today.
                    Joe
Waited until 3 pm.

John Rowe experienced enough unease to go straight to the nearest telephone box and dial 999. At 3.09 he left the message, 'There is something queer happening at Lloyds Bank at the junction of Wells Road and Broad Walk.'

After his foiled attempt to apprehend the disappearing car driver Rowe rang the police again to say:

'A rough looking man has just rushed out of the bank and driven towards the city in an Austin 16 car JHY 812.'

The police arrived to find George Barron Black dead.

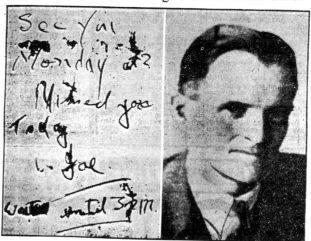

A police photograph of the note, presumed dropped by the bank killer – and his victim, George Black.

The car that Rowe had described had been reported as stolen that morning by its owner Mr F. Chappell, manager of Yeo Bros. and Paull, a company housed in a large building on the corner of Temple Way and Victoria Street. Mr Chappell always parked his car on a bombed site almost opposite his premises where he could keep an eye on it. At quarter past eleven that morning of January 7th, 1949, he noticed another car parked in his place. He rang the police at once and reported his vehicle as missing. Mr King, one of the sales staff remained in the trade counter area during the lunch hour and was convinced he saw his boss's car being driven past. The driver was tucked in close behind a van, obviously so that the policeman on point duty at Temple Gate would not observe and identify the registration number. Mr King immediately dialled 999.

A further sighting of the Austin took place in Bedminster between one and two o'clock. This witness took particular note as the driver seemed unused to handling the car. It was suggested that the car thief was accompanied by a woman at this point.

An acquaintance of Mr Chappell's saw the car parked outside a shop by the Broad Walk bank at around 2 o'clock and again half an hour later when there was a man in the driving seat. He thought nothing of it at the time, assuming that the driver was one of Chappell's staff.

The car was eventually found abandoned in Bellevue Road, Totterdown, shortly after the robbery. The murderer had vanished into thin air.

At the beginning of February an anonymous letter was sent to the *Bristol Evening Post* bearing the postmark of a 'town near Bristol'. The note was written in pencil on pale blue notepaper and was signed X29. It was handed to Chief Detective Inspector Melbourne Phillips who was in charge of the case. He allowed the *Post* to print the message although insisted that names and places be obliterated. It read:

Dear Sir, Trace up 'Blonde Lady' who went to _____ taking with her _____ June last _____ Large car, said her husband was a Detective before coming to _____ Swanked he always kept a gun about the house – sometimes took it out with him.

Gave address somewhere _____ Woman very tall and nice to speak to, in August this woman was seen on the terrace of the bowling green club with man in horn-rimmed spectacles, answers the wanted man in every way walking with _____ '

The letter went on to mention a possible link with the Odeon murder three years earlier and after the signature 'X29' was a postscript 'address and name of Blonde can be got no doubt from _____ man older than issued – 40 or 50.'

If the tall blonde was ever traced the enquiry obviously led nowhere.

In September of that year an armed robbery was attempted at the Midland Bank at Alston, near Penrith, in which the manager, 58-year-old Andrew Steele was shot dead. The assailant escaped in a taxi which was later found abandoned. The taxi driver, Ernest Ingram, appeared to have been killed prior to the raid and later the body of the robber himself was discovered. He had shot himself when he realized he was surrounded. He was identified as a 25-year-old ex-army officer, Charles Corbett Kennedy from Morpeth in Northumberland.

Three of the Knowle witnesses, Donald Twitt, John Rowe and Rev. Johnson were taken to Cumberland to view the body in the hope it could be proved that the dead bandit was the same man who had slain George Black but no satisfactory conclusion was reached and the file remained open.

Within months some of the stolen five pound notes began to turn up in various parts of the country and Bristol C.I.D. worked round the clock following up anything which might be deemed a lead. A reward of £1000 for information offered by Lloyds Bank attracted no takers. In 1955 Chief Detective Inspector Jesse Pane flew out to Italy to interview an Australian seaman called Ballantyne who came under suspicion but this turned out to be another dead-end.

In 1957 a raid took place on a bank in Mannheim, Germany by two men who killed a policeman and injured another in the process. One of the accused was an Englishman, Brian Cowell from Kent.

As it could be proved he was in this country at the time of the Knowle bank robbery, ballistics and finger print tests were taken in an attempt to establish a connection. But, no – another dead-end.

At the time the murder was committed police warned the public that, rather than be on the lookout for a 'ruthless murderer' they were more likely to find the respectably dressed young man had simply slipped back into his role as an ordinary citizen. There was speculation that an experienced criminal would have been unlikely to steal a car from a firm's car park in the morning and drive it round until he was ready to make his move in the afternoon.

His behaviour at the bank, too, was odd. In spending the entire afternoon waiting for the elusive Mr Murray he drew maximum attention to himself and he left behind fingerprints and the handwritten note which would suggest that he did not have a police record.

He was certainly a cool customer whose total confidence enabled him to single-handedly perfect the killing, robbery and successful escape. Where did he go? Did he flee the city, the country? Or is he still among us? He may even be reading this reconstruction now . . .

The Night of 'The Light That Failed'

R.N. Parrington Jackson, known to his many intimates as 'Jacko' was a handsome man with a sense of adventure. Before being appointed manager of Bristol's Odeon Cinema at the beginning of 1940 he had lived and worked in Hollywood, doing some film and radio work. One of his daredevil schemes was to drive from Los Angeles to New York with a pal – a distance of 3,500 miles – in five days.

He was immensely successful as a cinema manager. He was always immaculately attired in evening dress and had a talent for organizing personal appearance nights when stars would help raise money for charity, glamorous actresses such as Margaret Lockwood.

In the summer of 1940 he decided 'a man must do what he must do' and he signed on as a gunner in the Royal Navy. He served on the Prince of Wales and was present on board when Winston Churchill and Theodore Roosevelt signed the Atlantic Charter.

He survived the war and returned home to his wife and young son. They lived in Zetland Road. He took up his duties as cinema manager again in April 1946. He was 33 years old.

On Wednesday May 29th the film showing was *The Light that Failed* starring Ronald Coleman. The evening performance had just begun when staff in the restaurant area, which had closed at six o'clock, heard a shot ring out from the direction of the manager's office. The restaurant supervisor rushed in to find her employer lying on the floor by the doorway, blood streaming from a head wound. He was groaning and mumbling incoherently. Police and St. John's Ambulance men were on the scene in minutes and Mr Jackson was rushed to the B.R.I. where an emergency operation was carried out. In the meantime his wife had arrived at the picture house knowing nothing of the events which had taken place. She had just popped in to see her husband and catch the evening show.

The police broke the news to her and escorted her to the infirmary where she maintained a vigil at her husband's bedside. He died at 3.35 the following morning without being able to reveal the circumstances of the shooting.

Meanwhile at the Odeon the show went on, the audience totally unaware of the drama that had been played out behind the scenes.

The police were completely perplexed at the motive behind the murder or, in fact, how the killer had managed to melt away without being spotted.

Prior to the attack, Jackson had been laughing and chatting with the restaurant staff and had just returned from the box office with the takings when the incident occurred. None of the money had been stolen.

After the last patron had left at 9.30 p.m. the doors were locked and the staff interviewed but no one could offer anything that could be construed as a clue.

One man telephoned the police from the Odeon and was able to impart 'valuable information' which enabled the C.I.D. to issue a description of a man they wished to interview. He was aged 30–35, about 5′ 7″ and of medium build, with, it was thought, dark hair and a longish face with a ruddy complexion. He possessed 'tight or pursed lips' and was clean shaven. He was dressed in a dark suit, possibly navy blue which was well worn, even shiny in places. He wore a white collar and dark tie and had no noticeable accent. He had been sitting in the balcony lounge reading a newspaper.

Police enquiries spread to East Anglia and the Midlands, even America. Meanwhile the gun, a .45 revolver turned up in a static tank in the city. A year later they issued a statement saying they believed the killer stayed in Bristol for a few nights before committing the crime and that there were people who knew him who could reveal information if they chose. No one came forward.

Nearly thirty years later the *Bristol Evening Post* produced a sequel to this mysterious affair. Jeremy Brien, in 1975, wrote of Frederick Jesser who at that time was aged 73 and living in a Salvation Army hostel. Mr Jesser revealed he had given information to the police at the time of the murder describing a man in a dirty raincoat and cap who was sitting in the lounge at the top of the stairs when Jesser entered the circle with a companion.

It was Frederick Jesser's theory that Jacko was killed 'because he was too familiar with his staff' going on to say:

'Jacko was always the "hail fellow, well met" sort of bloke who would greet his usherettes, waitresses and kiosk girls with a hug or a kiss. It was nothing more than well-meant fun but I believe it led to one of their boyfriends becoming jealous.

'Something happened to one of the girls in the kiosk and although Jacko had nothing to do with it, he apparently got the blame.'

He said his suspect was aged between 20 and 30 but little of his face could be seen because of the cap he wore.

Well, could this have been the truth – that the suave, handsome cinema manager fell victim to a jealous swain? I suppose it could be as likely theory as any for such a seemingly pointless crime.

STOP PRESS [25.10.93]

As we go to print we learn that the Bristol police have been given the names of two men who carried out the murder. Their informant has told them that his father and a friend (both now dead) killed the cinema manager. A police spokesman is satisfied that the information is genuine and has asked witnesses and police officers who worked on the original case to come forward.

Horrific Happening in Horfield

Wednesday September 20th, 1950 began as an ordinary sort of day for Ethel Worth (née Mitchell) and her 40 year old son, Frederick. After he had departed for work (he was employed at the B.A.C.) she set about her household chores. She had been widowed three years previously and now rarely left the house. Ethel came from a well-known local family and had spent all her 65 years in the neighbourhood. Her youngest sister Gertrude lived nearby in Gloucester Road.

As usual, Fred came home at quarter to one for his lunch break. When he left after lunch to return to Filton, his mother was about to settle down in her favourite armchair for her customary afternoon nap, with the fire burning brightly in the living room hearth. Ethel poured herself a glass of water and placed it within easy reach on the mantelpiece for when she awoke.

When Fred returned at half past five there was no answer to his greeting, which he thought was odd. He pushed open the living room door and found his mother slumped in the chair, a woolly coat over her face. He first thought that she had suffered a stroke but when he approached her, Fred saw that she had been battered about the head and strangled. He immediately called in their G.P., Dr. Courtney who promptly contacted the police.

Det. Inspector Ivor Godden made the initial investigation at the scene of the crime. The wall by Ethel Worth's armchair and the chair itself was liberally splashed with blood.

The last person to see her alive, apart from the killer, was Harold Clarke, a disabled ex-serviceman of nearby Rozel Road. When he passed her house at two o'clock he saw her standing in her front room window and they had acknowledged each other with a brief wave. When he walked back down Hughenden Road 15 minutes later there was no sign of her.

Mrs Worth's next-door-neighbours at number 3 Hughenden Road were brother and sister, Harold and Lilian Woodfield. They had a married brother, Edward, aged 49 who lived in Southmead Road. Ted was on friendly terms with the Worths, mother and son, and had been known to borrow money from Ethel.

At 11.20 a.m. on Thursday September 21st, Det. Sgt. George Cox called on Ted Woodfield and acquainted him with the news of Mrs Worth's death. Ted replied, 'Oh, I'm sorry. That is the first I've heard about it.'

He then accompanied Det. Sgt. Cox to Police HQ where he was interviewed by Supt. Melbourne Phillips, who was in charge of the case. Ted was asked to account for his movements on the preceding day and he stated that he'd spent the afternoon in bed.

Supt. Phillips warned him to be careful, reminding him that Hughenden Road contained only a few houses and if he had been there at the relevant time it was quite possible that he had been seen by someone.

It was at this juncture Woodfield broke down and began to cry. After a moment or two he controlled himself, looked up from where he had buried his head in his hands said; 'It was a mad impulse. I will tell you.'

He then proceeded to recount the events of the previous day.

On the morning of the day in question he had received a reply to a letter he had written to his former employers, the B.A.C. Ted had asked for his old job back, which he had left in July for no apparent reason. But the B.A.C. were unable to reinstate him. His wife was later to tell the court that this letter seemed to depress him greatly and she was concerned at leaving him on his own when she went off to work that morning. He had been unemployed since leaving the B.A.C.

That morning, after his wife had left the house, Ted got himself ready and went to the Labour Exchange. On his way home he

22

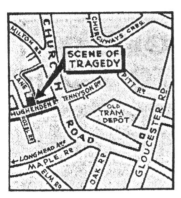

1 Hughenden Road, the scene of the killing of the 65-year-old widow.

23

stopped at a pub at the bottom of Chock Lane, Westbury-on-Trym for a couple of pints of cider, which he obtained for the princely sum of one shilling and fourpence.

Ted then returned home and got himself some dinner, deciding while he was eating to call on Mrs Worth and try to borrow some more cash. He was already in debt to her to the tune of £1.00. On his way out of his house he inexplicably picked up a lemonade bottle which he pocketed.

When Ethel Worth answered her front door to him he put his hand in his inside jacket pocket to give her the impression he was going to repay her loan. She invited him in and as he followed her down the hallway towards the living room he struck her on the head with the glass lemonade bottle.

Poor Ethel must have been totally bewildered and absolutely terrified at the turn events were taking.

'Don't Ted,' she pleaded as she sank into her armchair. He responded by hitting her again. Things were moving too fast for Ted Woodfield to stop now. Putting on a pair of his wife's gloves he just happened to have in his coat pocket, he clutched at the frail little lady's throat and squeezed the life out of her.

He then searched the house, taking money from the handbag she kept in the living room cupboard and a gold wrist-watch and field glasses from her bedroom.

He walked home across Horfield Common, abandoning the bottle and gloves on the way. He arrived back at Southmead Road at 4.20 p.m. He placed the watch in a cigarette case and buried it, together with the field glasses, by his back door. He then set about preparing tea for his wife, Katherine, who got back from her job at about five o'clock.

That night Ted Woodfield felt compelled to spend the fruits of his ghastly crime, knowing it was only a matter of time before the police were on to him. He took Katherine for a night out at the Beehive on Wellington Hill West. Little was she to know that it was to be the last evening she would ever spend in a pub in her husband's company.

The case came to court the following month and Woodfield's counsel, Mr J.D. Carswell KC entered a plea of insanity on his client's behalf. He described Woodfield as 'timid' and 'mild' and as being one who so 'hated the sight of blood' that a 'street accident would upset him badly.'

Katherine Woodfield and her husband's relatives all testified to the fact the Woodfield had never been known to lose his temper. Katherine, who had known him over thirty years, said 'He is the kindest man I have ever known,' while his sister announced him to be 'One of the best. I can't say anything against him.'

So what did cause this gentle man to act as 'a vicious beast' to quote the words used to describe him in court?

There was a history of insanity in his family, it is true. Both his grandmother and aunt had been inmates in Gloucester Asylum, and his mother suffered from delusions.

Some three years prior to the tragedy Woodfield had been examined and X-rayed by neurologists after experiencing some sort of attack when bending over. This had caused 'a click in his head' and he then suffered from double vision. He had been diagnosed as having hardening of the arteries and a blood clot on the brain.

There was a conflict of opinion among the medics called in to give evidence. Dr Gibson, for the defence, thought his condition could make him 'liable . . . to abnormally violent reactions in response to very small stimuli or upsets,' while Dr Hodge, for the prosecution, considered that although he 'might be more vulnerable to applied stress than the average individual,' Woodfield was, in his view, 'fully able to comprehend the nature and quality of his act and the consequences that would naturally follow.'

The jury returned a verdict of 'Guilty' and Edward Isaac Woodfield was sentenced to death. Appeals were lodged by his solicitor and by Dr Gibson but to no avail. The sentence stood and Woodfield was hanged, close to the scene of his crime, at Horfield Jail on December 14th, 1950.

So just how sane or insane was Ted Woodfield when he beat and throttled a defenceless pensioner who had shown him nothing but kindness for the sake of a few pounds, a gold watch and a pair of field glasses?

Slaughter at Stow-on-the-Wold

In 1834 Francois Jacques Rens was lodging at 'The George' in Stow-on-the-Wold. A former Hambro merchant, he had been ruined in the great commercial panic of 1825, the consequence of which was described as being 'an almost general breaking up of those who depended on paper money, and an approach to its utter annihilation.'

Through connections he had in Gloucestershire, Rens managed to find himself a post as Actuary of the Provident Bank at Stow. He was a good man, depicted as being 'gentlemanly, amiable, charitable and kind.' A creature of habit, he liked to take a stroll each evening between half past seven and eight o'clock. He carried with him a gold repeater watch, which struck the hour. It was attached to a brown silk guard and had a gold chain adorned with seals. He carried his money in a dark brown purse.

On the night of March 10th, 1834, the portly banker rose as usual

Rens lodged at The George, about one hundred yards from this church. (Local information was provided by Patrick Blagdon and his father Henry, who is one of Stow's oldest residents.)

26

from his chair, requested his hat and cloak be brought and vent into the chill March night. He was as regular in his habits · prized gold watch.

At quarter to eight Henry Sutton, a carter, saw Rens walking towards the horse pool in Back Lane.

Samuel Harris, a carrier, who lived about 40 yards from Back Lane, went to feed his horses at half past seven. As he was returning at eight o'clock he heard someone groaning. He found Rens lying on the ground and ran to the inn for help. Two others, Thomas Clifford and Charles Shepherd returned to the lane with him. Clifford, later describing the event said 'his head appeared beat and mangled to pieces.'

Francois Rens was carried back to The George and a surgeon Dr Robert Ryder Welch, was sent for. Fellow surgeon George Bulley Hayward lent his assistance as well. They both agreed it looked as if the man had been beaten with a bludgeon – in fact Dr Welch thought two separate weapons had been used. Rens had a large wound over the right temple, two on the back of his head and a number of smaller contusions. He remained unconscious until he died a little after midnight.

In April two men were arrested in connection with the crime, John Clifford and Richard Cox, and were tried at the next assizes. The evidence was circumstantial and they were deemed 'not guilty'.

Spring melted into summer and the first frosts of autumn were felt.

On September 19th, 1834 Edwin Jeffrey who worked for Richard Ellis, a butcher, brought a gold repeater watch to George Thornton, a tailor who repaired watches as a sideline. He told Jeffrey that 'it did not suit his [Jeffrey's] purpose' and the wily Thornton persuaded the young fellow to exchange it for a metal one. Edwin told him that he had bought the gold watch from his brother John when he was 'a gentleman's servant in Leamington Spa.'

Thornton, in his amateur way, took the watch apart, but unable to reassemble it, he took it to a professional, George Pain. Pain immediately recognised the watch as the one which had belonged to the benevolent banker. He handed the watch over to the authorities and Edwin Jeffrey was apprehended on September 26th. While in Northleach Gaol he made a confession.

He admitted that he had assaulted Rens at about eight o'clock on the night of March 10th and said he was the only person involved.

'Nobody told me to do it,' he said.

He had formulated the plan about a week or so prior to the event. He had watched Rens taking his customary stroll at the same time every evening and had vowed he would lay in wait one night and rob him. He had not intended to kill the man – all he wanted was his watch which he seemed to covet above all things.

On the night of the murder, Jeffrey took the stick his master used for stunning the calves and waited for Rens to pass by the back door of the Ellis house. He then followed him but when Rens circum-navigated the horse pool Jeffrey went straight to the gate of Mr Vavasow's field and waited there. Rens courteously wished the young man 'Goodnight' as he passed. As soon as the older man had gone a few paces Jeffrey came up behind him and struck him to the ground with one sharp blow. He snatched the watch and took the purse from his pocket. Rens was struggling on the ground and Jeffrey maintained that the other injuries were caused by Rens' struggle on the roadway.

Jeffrey made off with the spoils, hiding the watch in a neighbouring garden. He buried the timepiece, and covered it with mould, leaving a fraction of the chain showing so that he could identify the spot when he returned. He took the money out of the purse and pocketed it but lost the purse somewhere in the dark.

On returning in the direction of the stables Jeffrey spotted Samuel Harris coming down the lane so concealed himself until the man had passed. He returned the stick to its place in the slaughterhouse and then went to see to his horses, where he was joined by Lewis Huckings, Ellis's apprentice. Jeffrey said 'nothing to him then'. He went outside to check what time it was and saw William Richings in the alley near Ellis's house and was told that 'something was the matter' so he picked up the stable lantern and followed the other man. Rens had been helped into a nearby house and was propped up in a chair. Samuel Harris, Shepherd, the Eyford gamekeeper and Mr Pegler's groom were gathered round him, along with a man called William Roffe who went ahead to the inn to warn Rogers that they were bringing Rens back in a very bad condition. Jeffrey joined the party in carrying Rens back. By this time he 'was much alarmed and went back to the stable.'

When Jeffrey rejoined Lewis he told him what had transpired. They concluded their tasks and went back for their supper. They talked about the affair long into the night in the sleeping quarters they shared. Afterwards Jeffrey found he was unable to sleep.

Three days passed before the young butcher ventured back to the spot where he had concealed the watch. Cautiously glancing round he made certain no one was watching. It took him ten minutes to locate the hiding place. He decided to find a less conspicuous hidey hole, and chose 'the tallet. I put it on the side wall and put a piece of hay on it. About a month it lay there.'

After this passage of time Jeffrey deemed it safe enough to go and view his treasure every day and then to actually carry it around with him although, he said, he concealed it in his hand when anybody was present 'as I looked to see what o'clock it was.'

Then the watch started to go wrong and he took it to Mr Thornton. 'I never knew it would strike,' he says wistfully in his confession. His obsession with the shiny glittering article (he did not even realize it was gold) seems to have caused the act which had gained him the watch to pale into insignificance. He was like a magpie, single-minded in his quest. He never intended to kill Rens, he swore 'I had no malice or hatred against the man but merely a desire of obtaining his property.'

The money that had been in the dead man's purse amounted to eighteen pence which, to the best of Jeffrey's recollection he put towards 'paying the quarter due on my club. I belong to the Charlbury Club that meets at Stow.'

Jeffrey paid the highest price possible for his acquisitive nature when, on April 13th, 1835 he made his way to the gallows. He was allowed first to address the vast crowd which had assembled outside the prison. He cautioned them against 'frequenting beer-houses and against the breach of the Sabbath day', two factors to which he attributed his downfall. He had been urged to reveal whether or not he had an accomplice but expressed a desire 'not to be pressed further on that subject.'

Edwin Jeffrey, just twenty when he was hanged, was originally described by the press as being considered of low intellect but later those who had had a chance to study him more closely remarked 'he possessed considerable shrewdness and acuteness of understanding and he also had all the common rudiments of education.'

Did he really carry out the robbery and murder on his own? The impression is gained that he did not. Why then was he prepared to face the hangman alone? To whom did he owe such a great depth of loyalty? Alas, we shall never know.

The Arlingham Affair

Golden August days in Gloucester, 1873 seems an unlikely backdrop for murder as the cream of local farming society visited, entertained and went about their daily business. Nevertheless, that summer a violent crime of passion occurred which was to linger forever in the thoughts of all the families involved.

A string of farms line the road from Fretherne down to the Severn. Nearest the river stands West End Farm which in 1873 was run by Thomas Phipps. His sister Amelia Selina acted as housekeeper to him. It is said she resembled a golden haired china doll. Next along the way was Burcher's place, then Church Farm, which Charles Edward Butt (known as Edward) managed for his widowed mother. After passing Arlingham Church you would come upon the property occupied by James Merrett who was married to Thomas and Amelia's sister.

Edward Butt was absolutely besotted with Amelia. Although she was initially flattered by his attentions, by mid-August 1873 his possessiveness was beginning to irritate her.

Was the night of the Longney Feast the first time a serious rift occurred? The event took place on August 11th and Thomas, Amelia and Edward attended together to be met there by James Merrett and other friends. After supper the dancing began in a booth on the perimeter of an orchard.

Amelia danced all night, both with Edward and with other young men. She was young, pretty and popular and enjoyed the attention as any young girl would. Edward was angry. As they walked in the orchard for a breath of air at four the next morning, James Merrett heard him remonstrate with her and Amelia replied that it was not proper for a girl to dance with one man exclusively all night. Of course she was right. It would have been thought improper in those days unless a betrothal was imminent.

She was rather cool towards him in the days that followed, perhaps trying to impress upon him that she was not his property nor did she wish to be regarded as such.

The Arlingham Feast was scheduled for Monday August 18th.

West End Farm, Arlingham – little changed from Amelia's day.
(Photograph: Sue Lee)

Thomas had invited a friend of his, Harry Goddard, for the weekend. When this young man arrived on the Saturday night Amelia and Edward were in conversation at the garden gate. It must, indeed, have been difficult for Amelia to draw the thin line between politeness and encouragement with someone she had to meet on a daily basis.

Sunday, August 17th, dawned fine and warm. Thomas and Harry

set off at a little after nine for a walk and encountered Edward Butt en route. He returned to West End Farm with them. Amelia was in the kitchen preparing the lunch and Edward insisted on helping her string some kidney beans. Harry breezed into the kitchen and made some joking remark to which Amelia, her patience perhaps wearing a little thin, replied 'I didn't ask Edward to come and help and didn't want him.'

It seems she had come to realize it would take more than subtle hints to deter her swain and she would need to be blunter in her approach.

Other guests began to arrive, her brother Philemon, her cousin Richard Hill and a friend, John Webb. Amelia must have breathed a sigh of relief when Edward returned to his own farm for lunch.

That afternoon some of the party attended a service at Arlingham Church. Edward was standing by his gateway as Amelia passed by on the arm of her cousin Richard. He was still there when they strolled back in the Sunday sunshine so courtesy demanded they invited him back to tea. Was it then he noticed the attention Amelia was paying to Harry Goddard?

He must have been simmering still when the group paid a call on James and his wife in the early evening, especially when Amelia was teasing Harry and pulling his hair. A discussion arose about the transportation of some cheese to Gloucester the following day and James asked Amelia if she was going. Goddard said he would drive her and Merrett if she wanted to go and she accepted. Butt interceded by saying 'Amelia, if you go I'll take you,' to which she replied 'Harry has asked me first to go with him and James and if I go I shall go with them.'

This response must have incensed Butt and fuel was added to the flames when Amelia went into the orchard with Harry shortly afterwards and was missing for nearly half an hour. When they returned it was observed that Harry wore a flower in his lapel. A token from Amelia perhaps? Afterwards Harry said he could not remember.

Walking home in the dusk of the day Edward continued to pressurize Amelia to travel with him to Gloucester the next day. Later he was to state that she had previously promised that she would. Amelia remained adamant that she would travel with Merrett and Goddard and Butt came close to frustrated hysteria.

Merrett walked back with the others and Butt called into his own farm. He rejoined the rest of the party shortly afterwards. As some of the others were beginning to take their leave later in the evening Butt was seen in conversation with Amelia on the lawn. Merrett heard his sister-in-law call out 'James, James' and he hurried across to them. Amelia told him Edward had threatened to stab her. James lectured Butt on his stupidity but Edward refused to be detracted. 'You have deceived me, Amelia,' he complained. 'I have told you scores of times I should never have you,' she snapped back.

He repeated his entreaty that she travel with him to Gloucester and again she repeated the words she had used earlier. 'There'll be something bad the matter,' threatened Butt.

Merrett again attempted to mediate saying it was unlikely Amelia would trust herself to him after the incident at the Longney Feast to which Butt replied, 'What will my poor mother do, and the family?'

Not knowing quite what was meant by this remark Merrett led the pair back into the farmhouse and the three of them sat down, Butt and Merrett in the window seat, Amelia in a chair opposite.

Merrett spoke soothingly to Butt telling him he had 'as kind a mother and sisters as any young man in England, a good farm well stocked and everything to make him happy and comfortable.' Butt said 'Have I not managed it well?' Merrett then said there was 'no time lost for him or Amelia getting married.'

Butt repeated once again his request regarding the trip to Gloucester and again Amelia said 'No' so Butt flew into a frenzy once more, crying, 'I'll do as I told, I'll be damned if I don't.'

He said these words several times then grabbed Amelia by the arm and asked her to go outside with him. She acceded to his entreaty. Merrett accompanied them to the gate asking Amelia where Thomas was. She answered that he had probably gone to Mr Burcher's. Butt caught hold of Amelia by the arm and said 'Come with me, Amelia.'

As they walked up the road together Merrett heard Amelia say: 'I don't like one any more than the other, Edward; I shall talk to anyone.'

Almost immediately the report of a gun rent the night air followed by 'a rushing sound' like someone 'passing through a hedge'. Merrett ventured a little way up the roadway and found Amelia lying there. Half her jaw had been blasted away. Of Butt there was no sign. Amelia died shortly afterwards. It was now realized that when he had slipped back to his farm on the way back from the Merretts' house he had fetched his gun.

The following day Butt's clothes were found on the river bank.

Had he thrown himself into the water in a fit of remorse?

Amelia was buried at Whiteshill, her family home and the church and surrounding streets were thronged with mourners who wept for the beautiful girl whose life had ended so prematurely and tragically.

Charles Edward Butt was not dead. He had fled to Wales and was lodging near Abergavenny. There are two versions of how he was traced. Some say a letter to his mother was intercepted, others relate that one hot day he was cutting the hedge for his Welsh landlady and a prayer book fell from his jacket pocket when he removed it in the heat of the noonday sun. His name was inscribed on the fly leaf and, realizing this was a man on the run, wanted for murder, the landlady called the police. Whichever story is true he was arrested and brought to Gloucester to stand trial. His claim that the gun went off by accident was not believed by the jury and he was pronounced 'Guilty' and sentenced to death. He was 23 years old.

Throughout his stay in prison he kept a photograph of Amelia with him always and handed it to his mother before he went to face the hangman, saying he truly loved her. Local papers published a letter from him to Amelia's father asking his forgiveness and stating that he and Amelia were 'as man and wife'. Mr Phipps was furious at this slur on his daughter's reputation and had the newspaper publish a repudiation of this libel.

West End Farm has changed little since that August day when Amelia died so horribly. It is still owned by a branch of the Phipps family, Ken and Kathleen Jones. Up at Oldbury Farm live the Merretts, Mrs Diana Merrett being a member of the Burcher clan. The last of the Butts, Charlie, died a few years ago.

Assassination of an Aristocrat

The Thynne family, owners of Longleat, have a long and interesting history. Probably the wealthiest member of the clan was 'Tom of the Ten Thousand', so called because he was reputed to have an income of ten thousand pounds a year, a veritable fortune during the reign of Charles II. It was an age of extravagance and Thomas Thynne made many improvements to the home he had inherited from his childless uncle. He planted many trees on the estate and had a hard road laid out to Frome.

He formed a great friendship with Monmouth, the illegitimate son of Charles II, a result of the monarch's youthful liaison with Lucy Walter. Monmouth seems to have inherited his father's charisma and exerted his charm on everyone from the Queen herself to Charles' most famous mistresses, Barbara Castelmaine and Nell Gwynne. He was always in scrapes and was eventually banished from the kingdom, but he slipped back into the country and the soft-hearted king agreed to turn a blind eye provided Monmouth kept a low profile. Monmouth agreed and spent much of this period in Wiltshire with his friend Tom Thynne. The locals adored him which may have encouraged his later ambition to rule the country.

About this time, Tom Thynne's thoughts were turning to marriage and Monmouth suggested he could do worse than consider the beautiful, flame-haired Elizabeth Ogle who, although only 14 years old, was already a widow. The daughter of the IIth Earl of Northumberland, she had been wed at 13 to the Earl of Ogle, heir to the Duke of Newcastle, but he had died within the first year of their marriage.

Monmouth's machinations were successful and the betrothal was announced shortly after Elizabeth's fifteenth birthday. Elaborate preparations were made at Longleat to accommodate the young bride.

Elizabeth, however, had ideas of her own. Resentful at being a pawn in her ambitious family's game, she escaped to Holland before the marriage could be consummated. Upon arrival she took up residence with Lady Temple, the British Ambassador's wife.

Before her departure to the Continent she had made the acquaintance of the swashbuckling Count Charles John Königsmark who pursued her to Holland, declaring himself madly in love with her. Nothing was going to stand between him and the object of his desire and he made up his mind to rid himself of her inconvenient husband.

He came back to England, bringing with him his team of 'hit men' – A Captain Vratz, Lt. Stern, a soldier of fortune, and Boroskim, an impoverished Pole.

On Sunday February 12th, 1682, Thomas Thynne was in London, paying a visit to Elizabeth's scheming grandmother, the Dowager Countess of Northumberland, who lived near St. James' Park. It was dark when Thomas left the old lady's house. How soon did he become aware of galloping horses drawing level with his coach? Stern reined in his horse in front of Tom's carriage and Tom found himself staring down the barrel of Vratz's pistol. But it was Boroskim who fired – five shots from his blunderbuss. Although the injuries were to prove fatal, Thomas Thynne survived till the following morning and Monmouth was with him when he died.

Königsmark, a price of £200 on his head, disguised himself and attempted to flee the country by boat but he was captured, as were his confederates, and brought to trial. Königsmark managed to buy his way out of trouble by bribing the jury but the other three were condemned to death and died ignominiously on the gallows in Pall Mall, only yards from where the crime had been committed.

Monmouth stood and watched the execution. Lt. Stern protested strongly that he was dying for the sake of a man whom he had never met, for the sake of a lady and for a dead man whom he had never seen. The Pole declared he was only obeying orders. Only Vratz died bravely. His family had his body taken home to his native land where it was embalmed and put on public display for fifteen days.

News of Königsmark's disgrace had reached the Continent before he did and he decided to restore his good name by joining the Venetian service. He saw active service in Greece and was killed at the siege of Argos only four months after the murder, gaining nothing from his evil deed.

Monmouth also met a grisly death, being beheaded for his attempt to seize the throne.

The lady who had precipitated all the trouble went on to marry Charles Seymour, 6th Earl of Somerset. In later years she became a powerful political figure who had considerable influence over Queen Anne when she came to the throne.

The sometimes cruelly satirical Dean Swift circulated some scandalous verses about Elizabeth, insinuating that she had played a part in the plot to kill Thomas Thynne. She was so incensed by this that when Swift's name was put forward for the bishopric of Hereford she persuaded the Queen not to appoint him.

The murder of Thomas Thynne is depicted in bas relief in Westminster Abbey.

The Newent Enigma

The history behind the charge of murder levelled against Edmund Edmonds, a highly respected Newent solicitor, in 1872 contains the ingredients requisite of a television mini-series. It has it all – bankruptcy suits, allegations of illegitimacy, illicit liaisons and, of course, sudden death.

Our story actually begins many years earlier – in 1837 to be precise – when 21-year-old Ann Matthews of Boulsdon in Gloucestershire married 23-year-old Richard Legge, a tanner from Newent. Ann gave birth to a child two years later but, sadly, the infant did not survive. In fact the marriage only produced one offspring, a son, who lived to adulthood.

It cannot have taken Ann very long to realise she had not made an altogether wise choice of partner. Richard was 'wild and intemperate' and was soon to pay the price for his excesses. In 1843 he was brought home unconscious having suffered a stroke. He did, however, make a quite remarkably rapid recovery and progressed from being wheelchair bound to walking with the aid of a crutch in little over a month. By January 1847 he was out and about again.

His business affairs were in somewhat of a mess and Edmund Edmonds, then a solicitor's clerk, was endeavouring to sort matters out for him. He was frequently to be seen visiting the Legges and Richard's first outing on his recovery took him to Edmund's lodgings.

37

Ann Legge also used to call upon her husband's financial adviser, usually in the company of her sister, Mary (known familiarly as 'Polly') but sometimes alone. Now this rather outré behaviour was bound to cause speculation in early Victorian Gloucestershire and when a servant in Edmund's lodgings mentioned to people how scandalised she was, tongues began to wag. Ann's visits were made on Sunday afternoons when decent folk were at their worship in the local church and one evening when she was wending her way homewards at dusk she was set upon by members of the rougher element of the town's inhabitants who mobbed and insulted her.

On January 31st a Methodist church tea party was held at the George Hotel. Four hundred people turned up, paying one shilling per head. Richard Legge was well enough to attend. He was, apparently, in a state of intoxication and at some point in the proceedings removed his coat and challenged some innocent bystander to a fight.

Within a week or so, perhaps as a result of all this excitement, he was laid low with another stroke and had himself taken off to Chaxhill, for what reason was never told. April found him in Buolsdon where his wife's widowed mother lived. He died in June.

In October Ann gave birth to a daughter whom she named Mary Frances and the following June the child became beneficiary to a third of her grandmother's estate, Richard's mother, Caroline Augusta, having died intestate. The sum involved was nearly £4,500 – a sizeable sum in those days.

In October 1845 Ann married Edmund Edmonds.

On the last day of 1848 Mary Frances died aged four years and two months and the money held in trust for her reverted to her guardians, Ann and her new husband.

In November 1855 a suit was filed in Chancery to recover the money. It was alleged that Mary Frances was not the legal heir being, in fact, the result of Ann's extra-marital affair with Edmund. The point at issue was whether Richard could have been the father given his state of health at the time of the child's conception. Also were the letters purported to be from the widow Legge to her husband-to-be genuine? They gave clear indication that Edmund was Mary's father.

Eventually evidence that Richard Legge had been fit enough in January 1844 to visit Westgate Street in Gloucester to be fitted for a new suit of clothes seemed to indicate he was capable of siring a child

The George at Newent, the scene of the Methodist tea party. The Pigeon House, where Edmund and Ann resided, was demolished many years ago. The local library and a health club now stand on the site.
(Photograph: Tony Yeandle, present Licensee)

39

(though it is difficult to see the connection). This incident swung the balance and the Edmonds' retained the cash.

The couple settled back to life at Pigeon House, Edmund building up his business while Ann endured thirteen pregnancies. Four sons, Edmund, Oscar, Claude and Ralph survived although the two daughters, Ella and Gertrude, died in infancy. The rest were still-born. Not surprisingly, Ann's health suffered through this constant child-bearing. Her sister Polly had never married and lived with them as did Jeannette, Edmund's niece. She assisted him at the office. In 1867 she was seventeen years old. Her father was dead. Her mother lived at Ross-on-Wye.

On Sunday February 24th, 1867 Mr and Mrs Edmonds entertained Henry and Amy Symonds to supper. It seems Ann was feeling quite well that day, well enough to join Jeannette at the piano for a rendition of 'Too Late, Too Late' from 'The Ten Virgins', a sacred song so suitable for a Sunday evening. By one o'clock the following morning she was dead. The attendant physician, a close friend of the family, called Bass Smith, issued a death certificate stating cause as 'due to apoplexy.'

Five years passed and then suddenly the charge of murder was brought against Edmund Edmonds arising from statements made by Jeannette Edmonds, Bass Smith and others.

Why had they waited so long before dropping this bombshell? The reason given was that Jeannette was a minor under her uncle's protection and any allegations she might have made would probably have been suppressed. And Bass Smith? Here a rather lurid tale began to emerge. It transpired that Bass Smith, a married man and father of five, had made an assault on Miss Edmonds' honour on her seventeenth birthday. He had finally succeeded in seducing her the following year and they had been lovers from then until very recently.

The body of Ann Edmonds was disinterred and laid in the church. There it was viewed by the Coroner and the inquest jury. The body was almost mummified, 'the flesh being shrunk down to the bones and had become darkly discoloured and streaked with the yellow remains of the shroud.' The skull had been sawn through at the base of the forehead and removed by surgeons for critical examination. Many thought it should have been replaced 'to render full and complete the technical examination of the deceased by the jury.' As it was 'there was a hideous cavity in the head and for all purposes of ascertaining the cause of death, or arriving at any opinion in reference thereto, the inspection by the jury of the deceased lady was a useless and horrible exhibition.'

Jeannette Edmonds was the first witness sworn. She gave her address as the St James Diocesan Home in Hammersmith and was to recount a horrifying tale of events which she said took place on that February night in 1867.

She spoke of a quarrel which had broken out between husband and wife after the guests had left and the rest of the family had retired to bed. She heard Ann screaming and rushed downstairs to see what was happening. Ann passed her on the stairs and ran into Polly's room, her husband in hot pursuit. Jeannette followed them and heard Edmund cursing his wife who vowed she was dying. She said her uncle struck her aunt a blow to the head with his fist whereupon the poor woman sank to the floor stunned. She murmured a request for water which Jeannette fetched for her as Ann lay there holding her head. Edmund sped off to bring Bass Smith who injected her and bled her from the arm and temple and administered croton oil but all to no avail. Ann Edmonds died at one o'clock on the Monday morning. She was 51-years-old.

At the trial which followed Jeannette, by then aged 22 and described as 'of intelligent but by no means attractive appearance and dressed in somewhat fashionable style', told of her life at Pigeon House after the death of her aunt. She remained there up until October 1871. She was forced to admit to the 'criminal intimaces' she enjoyed with Bass Smith who, apparently, used to sneak back to the house after everyone else had gone to bed. Everyone, that is, with the exception of Aunt Polly who, according to Jeannette used to let the doctor in again thus implying that her aunt sanctioned Jeannette's illicit liaison. During the course of their affaire the doctor bought her expensive gifts and presented her with a photograph of himself. They called each other 'Anthony' and 'Cleopatra'. They sometimes stayed at Kenilworth as man and wife.

Jeannette told the court that she eventually left her uncle's house after an argument during which he slapped her about the head. When Bass Smith came to collect her belongings Edmunds refused to let them be taken away and ordered them to be brought down from the carriage on which they had been loaded. She testified that after her uncle had ordered her out of his house he discovered a half-written letter which she had begun to Bass Smith and had left in a desk drawer.

Dr Bass Smith backed up his mistress's accusation. He was closely questioned about his relations with Edmonds and forced to admit the man had attempted to have him struck off and had also handled a law suit against him which had left him bankrupt. He said that many times since Ann Edmond's death her husband had confided 'how sorry he was for his behaviour to his wife,' and on more than one occasion 'he has said that he felt he had murdered her by his unkindness'. After the funeral he alleged Edmonds said to him 'I know I have been a brute and a villain to her'. He insisted that on the night Ann died he had questioned Polly as to whether there had been any violence that night as he knew there had been in the past.

Philip James, the carpenter who had provided the coffin and his wife, Ann, who had made the shroud, both said they had noticed a wound on the deceased's forehead when they called early on the Monday morning, February 25th. Dr Smith was bathing it with a sponge, they said.

Elizabeth Davies, a dressmaker, had called at the Edmonds' residence on March 1st and had asked if she might see the body and pay her last respects. She had immediately noticed a bruise on the forehead and had asked Jeannette how it happened. Jeannette had answered by saying it was caused by a handkerchief being tied round her head.

Ann Bradd who had been a servant at Pigeon House at the time gave her testimony with great confidence. Since the death, she told the court 'I have been roving and unsettled.' She recalled the day Mrs Edmonds had died. She told of the supper party and remarked that Mr Edmonds was extolling the beauty of a Miss Smallridge. After she had gone to bed (she slept in the Nursery) she heard a commotion downstairs and the sound of something heavy being thrown. She thought it may have been a candlestick. She confirmed Jeannette's story of the screams and the flight upstairs but said that prior to this, Mrs Edmonds had run out into the garden. She attested to the stormy relationship between the Edmonds' and swore the reason she had not told the truth when faced with an inquisition by Ann's mother just after the event was because Polly had instructed her 'Hannah, you know what an excitable woman your mistress was. Do not say anything about her death.'

She admitted to mentioning her misgivings to the coachman, Arch, a week or so after the tragedy but forebore to record his reaction. She eventually left Mr Edmonds' service in August 1867 after an argument.

Mr Digby Seymour, Counsel for the Prosecution, asked the jury to consider in her favour what possible motive she could have had in coming forward at this time.

Edmund Edmonds was called to the stand and swore under solemn oath he had not struck his wife. He said she had been in poor health for a number of years and had complained of head pains over a long period. He stated that in 1866 Bass Smith had expressed the opinion that one day she would die suddenly. Edmonds insisted he had found Jeannette's half-written letter to her lover on October 9th the previous year, prior to her departure. He was already irritated with her, this he readily admitted, as she had made a great many mistakes that day in some work he had set her to do. This, combined with the shock of reading the letter and all it implied, had enraged him to such an extent that he slapped her. She left the next day and he forebade her to take all her possessions, possibly because he had paid for them.

He spoke frankly of the argument he had had with Smith when he came for Jeannette's boxes but denied every saying anything which could have been considered as an admission that he had 'murdered his wife by unkindness.'

He was closely quizzed about his pre-marital relations with Ann and also as to whether he was on intimate terms with his sister-in-law Polly who had just turned forty at the time of the trial. He denied any improper behaviour with either woman and said firmly he had never struck his wife 'since they had lived at Pigeon House'.

At the inquest he was asked if he knew his brother Henry had gone to London with the express purpose of removing Jeannette from the Home and also whether he had knowledge of Polly's trip to Powick the previous Sunday in an abortive attempt to track down Ann Bradd. He had to admit, yes, he had known.

The first Defence witnesses were Henry and Amy Symonds, who had supped at the Pigeon House a few hours before Ann's death. They both averred there had been no sign of discord between the couple. They were followed to the stand by Ralph Edmonds, the second son who confirmed this and stated his parents lived happily together.

Ann Arch, who as Miss Cassidy had worked for the Edmonds' prior to her marriage to the coachman, John, also painted a picture of marital harmony. Both she and her husband were decisive in their denial that Ann Bradd had ever voiced any suspicions to either of them regarding the circumstances of Mrs Edmonds' death.

The same story was borne out by Mary Coborne Edmonds, Jeannette's sister, who had taken the place of the disgraced girl at Pigeon House. Polly then took up the tale and gave her version of the events of the fatal night. She said she heard no screams or Ann crying out 'Don't – there's a dear man, don't'. Oscar, now fifteen and a student at Malvern College, had been in the room at the time and backed up her story.

It was probably Polly Matthews' testimony which ensured Edmonds' eventual acquittal. It is also more than likely that Jeannette's scandalous affair with the doctor coloured the view of the jury with regard to her evidence and made them doubt the credence of anything she said. The same would be true of Bass Smith's deposition. The whole body of evidence was a mass of contradictions and even the judge Mr Baron Bramwell, in his summing-up professed he could see no reason why Ann Bradd should have lied or, if she were in cahoots with Jeannette, why they had not made sure their stories had coincided with more accuracy. He also made a point regarding Edmund's presence in his sister-in-law's room on the night in question. 'It was strange,' he commented, 'that a man should go into an unmarried female's room when she was in bed, even if his wife were with him.'

There were a great many strange features appertaining to the case and, indeed, the whole life style of the family. The promiscuity, both implied and proven, was certainly somewhat avant-garde in an era where morality and respectability were supposed to have ruled.

So who was telling the truth? Or was no one telling the complete truth?

The jury reached a 'Not Guilty' verdict in less than fifteen minutes and this decision was greeted 'with some applause' causing a reprimand from the Bench.

One is left wondering what became of them all. Did Edmund marry the loyal Polly? What became of Jeannette? And Bass Smith? Bankrupt and with his career in ruins did Mrs Smith forgive him his peccadillos?

The whole business is totally fascinating in the glimpse it gives us of small-town Victorian life 'behind the net curtains' as it were but it does leave many questions unanswered.

Nemesis

The story of Luke Heath and Sarah Harris is in the classic 'squire's son/peasant girl' tradition although Luke's father was actually 'a respectable farmer' rather than a squire.

The setting for this early nineteenth century rural tale is a Gloucestershire village with the romantic name of Cow-Honeybourne. Sarah lived with her father in abject poverty in a cottage about a quarter of a mile from the Heath residence. Her two older sisters were married and living in the village.

Luke Heath was 24 years old when he cast his lustful eye on Sarah. He insisted their meetings be clandestine explaining to her that her father would not 'sanction his addresses'. A more probable reason for the secrecy was Luke's certain awareness that James Harris would immediately realize that the young man's intentions were less than honourable.

Initially the two met in what is described in contemporary accounts as 'the pent house' which, in modern parlance, conjures up the picture of a luxury apartment but, of course, the original meaning is intended here – 'a building, separate to the house, with roof aslope' – in other words a shed or outhouse. This, then, was the couple's trysting place.

This arrangement did not really suit the lascivious Luke's design as he was planning a full-scale seduction so, with honeyed words, no doubt, he persuaded young Sarah to smuggle him into her bedroom. Now, given the layout of the cottage, this was no easy task. The cottage was exceedingly small and seems to have consisted of little more than three rooms in a straight line. On entering the abode one would come first into the kitchen and have to pass through Sarah's room to that in which James slept. Wily Luke oiled the door hinges so that James would slumber on blissfully unaware of the scenes of torrid passion in the adjoining room.

Needless to say, it was not long before the inevitable came to pass and Sarah found herself pregnant. She confided her condition to her married sisters (although not to her father) and began to apply pressure on Luke to make an honest woman of her.

The chapel at Cow-Honeybourne. Since the alteration of the county boundaries, this village is now part of Hereford and Worcestershire.

Did Luke pretend that he would wed her? Quite probably he did, but that was not really in his scheme of things. She had been an amusing plaything but marriage was a different kettle of fish and would hardly find favour in his family's eyes.

What thoughts were running through Sarah's head on that balmy June night, Midsummer, 1809? As she waited for her lover was she praying that by the time her father noticed her condition arrangements for the wedding would be finalised?

The following morning James Harris arose and, passing through his daughter's bedroom on his way to the kitchen, was surprised to notice she was not in her bed. He wondered if, unusual as it might be, she had gone into the garden? The back door was ajar and he stepped outside, almost stumbling over a pitchfork which lay across the path. Of Sarah there was no sign.

Feeling something must surely be amiss he walked to the village and knocked at the door of the cottage where his eldest girl lived. Sarah was not there but he did learn for the first time of Sarah's pregnancy and also the identity of the father. Thoroughly alarmed, he proceeded to his other daughter's place, hoping against hope that Sarah was there. He returned to his own home to be met with the news that Sarah's body had been pulled from the pond which was less than sixty yards from his door. She had been viciously attacked with the very same pitchfork which lay on the path and on which James could now see the stains of his daughter's blood. There was a wound on her temple and a hole in the back of her head.

Naturally the finger of suspicion pointed at Luke who was apprehended on his father's farm. He denied all knowledge of the murder. He attended the coroner's inquest but no solid evidence was unearthed to implicate him and he was acquitted. Within days new evidence came to light and a warrant was issued for his arrest. But it was too late, the bird had flown. His father's farmhouse was searched and although nothing incriminating was found, the fact that he had disappeared told against him and was taken as proof of his guilt.

A search was ordered and the country combed but after three fruitless months the manhunt was abandoned. It seemed the perpetrator of the brutal slaying of young Sarah Harris would never be brought to justice.

Four years passed before the whereabouts of Luke Heath were discovered. He was living at the time as a farm servant in Kidderminster under the name of 'Farmer John'. He was taken into custody. He denied all knowledge of Sarah Harris or her family and swore he had never lived in Gloucestershire but when the name of 'Cow-Honeybourne' was mentioned a change came over him. He hid his face in his hands and shook with agitation as the tears coursed down his cheeks.

He was questioned as to his movements before taking up residence in Kidderminster two years earlier and he stated he had been aboard a man-of-war. This, however, was later proved to be a lie.

While on remand in Kidderminster Gaol he confessed to a fellow prisoner that he had made Sarah pregnant and had killed her with a pitchfork. He begged the other man to keep silent about what he had said but, of course, the request was ignored and probably won some felon a lighter sentence.

Luke Heath was transferred to Gloucester Gaol. He remained impassive throughout his trial. He was found guilty, thereafter he made a full confession and appeared 'duly penitent' at the end.

He was executed at Gloucester Gaol 'On the Drop over the Entrance Lodge' on Monday August 30th, 1813.

'Cook was a Lively Girl . . .'

The story of William Walter Burton and Winifred Mary Mitchell acted out, as it was, in the sleepy Dorset village of Gussage St. Michael in the year before the First World War started, reads like a novel by Thomas Hardy. Even their professions add to this illusion – they were both employed by Mr Good who lived at Gussage Manor and farmed many acres in the district – Burton was a rabbit trapper and Winifred was the cook.

William Burton was 29 years old, a tall, well-built, athletic man with a fresh complexion, grey-blue eyes, brown hair and a long, sandy moustache. He sang in the church choir and was among the team of bell-ringers. He was married to Lily, a woman a little older than himself. Lily was the village postmistress and she also assisted at the village school. The couple had a child and lived at the Post Office which bordered on the Sovel Plantation.

Winifred was 24. She was pretty and petite with dark hair. According to Burton she was 'a lively girl and liked plenty of fun and she would say anything.' Her parents lived in nearby Manswood and she had previously worked in Bournemouth which may have caused her to be a little sophisticated by village standards. She was a distant relative of Burton's stepmother.

Friendship blossomed between the pair which soon led to a full-blown affaire d'amour. Passionate letters were exchanged and gifts of gold jewellery were showered on the attractive young cook. Various items of female clothing were charged to Burton's account at 'Alexander and Cherry's drapery establishment'. Her presents to him were less lavish and seemed to amount only to a penholder which he kept on his mantelshelf at home.

The course of a clandestine romance rarely runs smoothly, particularly if one of the partners is a single girl and the other a married man. Expensive trinkets and secret meetings are all quite exciting but being in her mid-twenties Winifred had to contemplate her future security and look for a long-term relationship. She began to try to persuade William to elope with her to Canada. As men of his ilk so often do, he tried to dodge the issue but she became more persistent. Winifred told him she feared she was pregnant and if he reneged on his promises she would be forced to apprise his wife of his misdemeanours both with herself and other girls.

Just what promises did Burton make to encourage her to dress up 'in all her best things' on the afternoon of Monday March 31st, 1913? She put on her long coat and a veiled hat, gloves and a fur boa. Round her neck she fastened a locket on a gold chain and she put on her gold bracelet, dress ring and brooch. She lunched at two o'clock and just before three set off for the village on her bicycle, pausing for a chat with Lily Burton on her way. Did she feel a perverse sense of triumph as she smiled sweetly at her lover's deceived wife?

Shortly afterwards she was seen chatting with Burton himself. He sat on some rails while she stood by her bicycle. She was never seen alive again.

Prior to his meeting with his paramour, he had approached young Leonard Mitcham and asked if he might borrow his father's gun and a few cartridges as he wanted to shoot 'Boyt's black and white cat'. This request being granted, he walked a little way with the boy and enquired of him:

'Len, do you think that if I got up close to anyone with this gun, it would kill them?'

'Yes, of course it would,' Len answered.

'It would blow their head all to pieces?' persisted Burton.

'Yes,' replied Len.

The gun was returned at five o'clock that day with one cartridge spent, but that cartridge had not found its way into Boyt's cat as that feline still stalked the village. Burton exhorted Len not to mention to anyone that he had been in sole possession of the gun all afternoon but rather that the two of them had strolled to the top of the hill, fired a couple of shots and had come down again.

Later in the evening Burton approached Boyt himself and asked him to walk up with him to the Sovel Plantation as he had three traps to see to. They walked up the bridle path and Fred Boyt waited while Burton went in to the plantation. He returned within five minutes pushing a lady's bicycle. He told his pal that the machine was Winnie's and he had to take it back to Manswood for her as she had gone to Canada. The two men walked over to Manswood and duly deposited the bike. As they made their way back to Gussage St. Michael Burton remarked ominously; 'If you ever mention about me pushing back the bike it will be a bad job for you.' Boyt, knowing

Burton to be a man of his word, took the threat seriously and adhered to Burton's instructions. Several times over the next few days Burton reiterated the command.

Throughout those first few days of April 1913 Burton told a variety of stories regarding Winifred's whereabouts and insisted that her family had heard from her. At the end of the month he announced to an acquaintance, Ernest Fry:

'Cookie's found then!'

'Is she?' Fry was amazed.

'Yes,' Burton went on, 'in London. I did not think that she was gone to Canada and I should not be surprised to see her back here before long.'

On April 30th the mystery of the vanishing 'Cookie' was solved. George Gillingham, a dairyman who also worked for Good, handed over to Police Sergeant Stockley part of a denture which he had found while walking in the Sovel Plantation with his wife some weeks previously and which had been on his mantelshelf since. Things then began to slot into place as other pieces of evidence came to light.

There was the strange discovery by Henry Palmer and his friend Raymond; the boys had been gathering primroses up on the plantation on the day before Winnie's disappearance when they had come upon what looked to them like a newly-dug grave.

Winifred Bailey, another servant at the Manor House, who had shared a room with Winnie, confided that she had been used as the couple's go-between and that some time after the unexplained flight Burton had said, 'It's a funny thing where she has gone to. I will take my oath I have done nothing to her. If the police find her in the plantation she has been killed away and brought there for someone else to take the blame.'

On May 1st Police Sergeant Stockley searched Winnie's belongings and found some torn up papers which, when pasted together, proved to be two letters from Burton to the vanished girl. The following day he went up to the Sovel Plantation with P.C. Light and young Henry Palmer, who pointed out the location of what had seemed to be a grave. They set to work with shovels and soon the body of Winifred Mitchell surfaced. She was lying face down and when the two officers turned her over it was revealed that half her face had been shot away. She wore all her gold and her veiled hat but some of her clothes were missing and her long coat was wrapped round her.

Burton was arrested immediately and proclaimed, 'I shall be blamed as I was the last one that was seen with her.' He began to cry. He was taken to Cranborne Police station where he expressed regret that he had ever got mixed up with Winnie. He said, 'The only one I worry about is my wife who is as good a woman as any man can have.'

After being in custody for two days Burton made a statement regarding his movements on the afternoon in question, making no mention of seeing Winnie after three o'clock. He concluded by saying, 'If some men would come forward they could clear me.'

Unfortunately for Burton everyone who did come forward had only damning statements to make. An old friend of the prisoner, Arthur Bush, a labourer from Cashmoor, testified he had several conversations with Burton regarding Winnie's sudden exit. Burton confessed to Arthur that he had been on intimate terms with her and was afraid she was 'in trouble' and he wished he could get 'some young man to take her so as to shift the blame from me.'

Mr Justice Ridley, the judge presiding at Burton's trial, on several occasions used the adjective 'atrocious' in connection with the crime which had been 'inhumanly cruel in its cold and calculated premeditation.'

Burton had certainly planned elaborately for the elimination of the pretty plaything who had turned into a threat. He had organized the grave-digging on the previous day so that he would be seen about the village on the fatal afternoon and it would appear he had not had time to bury his victim in the time allotted.

Two days before the slaying Burton had talked to a friend of his called Fred Butt 'I know you can keep a secret, Fred,' he had said, proceeding to confide that Winnie had made arrangements for the two of them to elope. Butt, being a thoroughly respectable and moral man had urged him not to embark on such a foolish course.

Had this well-meaning advice been the deciding factor in determining that the pretty young cook must die? In his confession Burton admits 'I was proper led away by her,' but totally panicked when she began to pressurize him to run off with her. In respect of her death he states, 'The poor girl did not suffer anything. She fell dead in an instant and did not speak.'

After bidding farewell to his distraught wife, William Burton walked with great composure to the Dorchester gallows on Midsummer Day 1913.

A Lily of the Field

It was half past seven on the morning of April 15th, 1950 that the body was found. Mr Moate, who lived at Kitbury Farm, near Bridgwater, glanced out of the window and saw a shape in one of the fields. He thought it might be an injured sheep and sent his 6-year-old son, Richard, to investigate. He watched the boy approach the object, pause, then race back towards the house. When he went out to see what had caused his son to panic the lad said it was a body lying there and it was badly injured. Mr Moate set off immediately to check on this but meanwhile Mrs Davey, wife of a smallholder of West Street in Bridgwater, had stumbled on the corpse as she and her husband were on their way to milk the cows. The body was that of a young woman, naked but for her shoes and stockings. She had been the subject of a ferocious attack and her head was horribly battered.

The body was soon identified. The young woman was Lily Irene Palmer, daughter of Cyril and Rose Palmer. She had lived with her parents at 36, Kidbury Road and was 26 years old. She was a slim, fair-haired girl whom everyone agreed was possessed of a pleasant nature. She had held various jobs – she had been a factory worker and worked in a domestic capacity although she had been unemployed for the last six months of her life. Her last job had been with the Quantock Preserving Company. Three years previously she had been interviewed by a mental health worker and there had been some talk of her being admitted to Sandhill Park Hospital, a centre which dealt with people with mental problems but nothing more had transpired on this score.

Her parents explained that she often came in late at night. They always left a key outside for her so they were unaware that she had not returned on the fatal evening. People in the locality were later to say they heard dogs barking at around eleven o'clock and it was initially thought the attack took place then, although on examining further evidence it would appear that it might have been slightly earlier.

Police trying to piece together the last hours of her life established

52

that she spent the evening in a pub in town called 'The Horse and Jockey'. Her companion had been a 24-year-old man by the name of Ronald Atwell.

Det. Sgt Crocker and Acting Det. Sgt Lockyer called at the Gasworks in Old Taunton Road just before lunchtime that day to speak to Atwell who was employed there. After a brief interview he was arrested and taken to Bridgwater Police Station. He made a statement and at 6.00 p.m. he was charged with murder.

Although at the outset Atwell insisted Lily had left the pub while he was in the skittle alley, he finally admitted that they had left the hostelry together at about 9.30 p.m. They had walked through Dursley Road and Northfield Road to a spot near Wembdon Church where a footpath ran across the fields. He said he had been quite sober having had only two or three pints of beer. Lily had had two glasses of beer.

He then stated they paused in one of the fields and he asked Lily to take off her clothes. As she acceded to his request he began to rain blows on her. 'I must have gone off my nut,' is how he phrased it. He lost his temper and struck her in the face with his fist several times. He thought he might also have put his hands round her throat. As she collapsed on the ground he kicked her repeatedly. He then realized he must have killed her and bent down and felt for a pulse. There was none. He hesitated a moment or two beside her lifeless form then walked back to his home in nearby Kendale Road. Witnesses saw him approach this road from the direction of the meadow at about 10.45 p.m.

He told the police he had every intention of contacting them during his lunch break the following day had they not forestalled him by calling on him instead.

A prison surgeon who examined Atwell gave his opinion that the young man was mentally unstable although not certifiable. He considered it feasible that Atwell had lost control of himself when he launched the frenzied attack and was not fully aware of what he was doing for at least part of the time.

It was not the first time Atwell had found himself in trouble of this nature. Only weeks before Lily's death he had been found guilty on a charge of drunkenness and an assault on a young woman. On this occasion Atwell had approached the girl from behind and had put his hands round her throat. In the light of later events this girl had got off lightly.

53

Ronald Atwell.

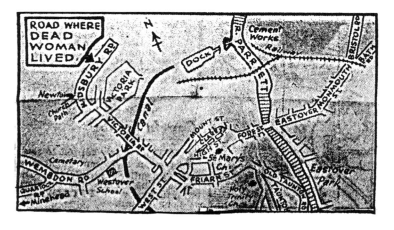

Atwell lived with his aunt and uncle, Philip and Minnie Pear. According to them, he had suffered a fall at the age of four, and had sustained a blow to the head which had left him with rather unstable behavioural patterns. His uncle said the boy would 'go into a dream without being asleep,' and that his mental state had deteriorated rapidly in the past year after a double bereavement – first his grandmother had passed away and then the girl he had hoped to marry died suddenly. After these tragedies he became very moody and began to neglect his appearance.

Ronald Douglas Atwell was smartly dressed, however, when he appeared in the dock at Wells Assizes on May 31st, 1950. He pleaded 'Not Guilty'.

The jury heard a description of Lily's ghastly injuries; there had been a wound an inch and a half long on her forehead, part of one ear was missing, her nose was broken, her eyes blackened and her false teeth smashed. She suffered a massive haemorrhage to the neck and to the left side of her brain.

It took the jury a mere ten minutes to reach the verdict of 'Guilty'. Atwell reacted by raising his eyebrows slightly and giving a half-smile. He was executed at Horfield Jail in July of that year.

A particularly sad note to this unhappy tale is the description of Lily's black and white mongrel dog to whom she was devoted. The poor little thing could not understand why she did not return. He sat outside her house the whole of the following day refusing to move until she came back.

Brutality in Bull Lane

The demise of Eleanor Bunt is one which contains all the facets of which drama is formed – love, jealousy and murder. The setting for this story is a dark, narrow dwelling in Gloucester's Bull Lane off busy Westgate Street, a section of which still remains huddled between modern office blocks and car parks. The year was 1741.

Eleanor Bunt was a stern, miserly woman who employed just one servant, a girl from the Forest of Dean. The girl's name was Mary Palmer. Mary had to work extremely hard and to live by Mrs Bunt's strict rules, the most important edict being 'no followers' – that is to say Mary was not permitted a boyfriend. Perhaps when she took the job she was quite willing to abide by this principle but when her eyes met those of Henry Sims across the counter at Shorts, the Linen

Drapers in Westgate Street such pledges were soon forgotten. Henry fell in love with the pretty country girl and she with him.

It was unfortunate for Mary Palmer that Henry was the object of another woman's desires. Had Miss Jones who worked on the same counter cherished hopes that he felt the same way towards her? Had he ever offered her any encouragement before his eye fell on Mary?

Miss Jones seethed with jealous rage as she watched the man of her dreams gaze fondly at his new love. She whispered maliciously to all and sundry that Henry was courting 'Mrs Bunt's servant' and the couple were forced to discontinue meeting for a while fearing Mary's job would be in jeopardy. Miss Jones' hopes were raised by this development but were to be cruelly dashed as she spotted Mary pass by the window one day and saw Henry's face light up with a loving smile as he discreetly blew his adored one a kiss.

It was not very long before a 'well-wisher' acquainted Mrs Bunt with the situation by means of a note pushed under her door. Mrs Bunt, immediately upon receipt of this missive, donned hooded cloak, mittens and muff, called Mary and led her to the shop in Westgate Street. There she requested words with the manageress, Miss Johnson. In due course Mary was summoned to the office and her indiscretions catalogued and Mr Sims' character discussed. Miss Jones was sent for and Mrs Bunt invited her to call at the house in Bull Lane that evening.

Miss Jones did as she was bid and was delighted to witness a storm of abuse directed at the hapless Mary. Mrs Bunt threatened to cut her out of her will. Mary lost her temper and answered back. It seemed her dismissal was imminent and Miss Jones must have felt it would not be long before she had a clear field with regard to Henry Sims. She watched and waited and several days passed by without any sign of Mary leaving town. Miss Jones silently fumed. She began to notice that Henry was acting in a rather preoccupied manner. One day he seemed particularly nervous. As closing time approached she saw him slip out through the back door and sneak through the garden with an air of great secrecy. She crept out in his wake and saw him scale the wall at the bottom. She pressed herself close to the wall and could make out a whispered conversation in progress. Unable to hear what was being said she climbed on a cask which stood by the wall. Thus she was able to eavesdrop on the lovers' meeting.

Mary, who must have been as practical as she was pretty, was

Bull Lane, in the nineteenth century, looking away from Westgate Street.

explaining to Henry that it would never do to cross Mrs Bunt so they must be ultra-cautious and meet only infrequently until the day she inherited her promised 'fortune' – her legacy of £50. With the money, pointed out the sensible girl, they could buy the sole shop in Little Dean, her native village, at present owned by her uncle. As Mary described the idyllic prospects the future held for them both Henry admitted to wishing they had the money here and now.

Miss Jones crept back to the shop. She scuttled off to Bull Lane at the first opportunity to repeat the conversation to Mrs Bunt hinting that Mary was, in all probability, planning to murder her mistress. Mrs Bunt declared she would dismiss the wretch at once.

Miss Jones scurried home with a happy heart yet she did not sleep easy in her bed that night. Was it her conscience or merely the ferocity of the terrible storm which raged on that night, September 19th, 1741? All night long the wind howled in the treetops and tore tiles from roofs; thunder claps echoed in the sullen sky. As the gales abated and a pearly light crept across the clouds from the streets came a more fearful sound – that of human voices crying 'Murder, Murder'. People began to run towards Bull Lane.

Eleanor Bunt was dead, murdered in her bed. She had died in a welter of gore from the ghastly wound in her throat. The room was in chaos, clothes scattered on the floor, drawers and cupboards ransacked. No sign of forced entry could be detected – all the doors and windows were securely fastened. The only incriminating bloodstain was a smear on the handle of Mary's door. Protesting her innocence the girl was hauled off to gaol. Henry Sims was also arrested, at the instigation of the vindictive Miss Jones, but was discharged after a single interview.

Mary remained in prison for many dreary months, for the Gloucester Assizes were scheduled for March at the end of the Spring Circuit. Henry visited her constantly and attempted to convince anyone who would listen that the girl he loved was completely innocent of the dreadful crime.

At last the trial came to court and the events of that storm-wracked night and its aftermath were detailed. The actual discovery of the body took place at six o'clock on the morning of September 20th. The butter woman from Turgworth had rung the house bell twice before it was opened by Mary in a half-dressed state. In retrospect it was said she seemed confused. She told the butter woman she had no money but would go and fetch some from her mistress. She ran upstairs and re-appeared very rapidly crying out that Mrs Bunt was murdered. She ran into the street screaming then passed into a dead faint.

Miss Jones was amongst the throng who surged to Mrs Bunt's front door but everyone was too afraid to enter until the constable arrived.

Miss Jones' evidence regarding the quarrels and the discussion she overheard were duly noted in Mary's disfavour although the missing gold, jewellery, watch and plate was not found on the premises. The judge pointed out to Mary's credit that she did not flee the scene of the crime so did this not suggest she could have been innocent?

There was a deathly hush throughout the court room when the jury pronounced their verdict. When 'Guilty' was heard a buzz of reaction was drawn from the spectators and Mary herself collapsed in tears crying for mercy and declaring she did not do the deed. She was carried back to the cells unconscious.

Three days later Mary was taken to the scaffold still swearing her innocence.

After the judicial death of the woman he loved Henry Sims left Gloucester and went to work in Stroud, a desolate and bitter man.

Two years passed by and then a gang of villains were apprehended in Cirencester on charges of burglary and forgery. One of the prisoners, under sentence of death, confessed to the Bull Lane murder. The details were then revealed, of how the desperadoes had gained access to Mrs Bunt's house via an empty building opposite. They had stretched a plank across the narrow street and climbed across, entering her home by the garrett window. The crime committed, they had deliberately smeared the handle of the servant's room to cast suspicion upon her before stealthily returning the way they had come, carrying with them their ill-gotten gains. The roar of the tempest drowned any sound they may have made.

These revelations caused an uproar in Gloucester. Miss Jones was forced to leave town and the officiating magistrates came under fire. Mary Palmer's remains were removed from their rough grave in the prison yard and re-interred in a coffin which was carried on a plumed hearse in procession throughout the city headed by the faithful Henry Sims as chief mourner. She was buried in hallowed ground in a tomb paid for by the dignitaries of the city. In an attempt to atone for their dreadful mistake a public proclamation of Mary's innocence was given out by the Mayor and magistrates as well as all the money lavished on the extravagant funeral but all their words and cash could not resurrect the country girl who had lost her life because of a miscarriage of justice.

'Her Mother is No Good . . .'

In 1932, when she was only fifteen, Violet Kathleen Smith started 'walking out' with farmer's boy Reginald Woolmington, a well-built athletic young fellow who was a keen amateur boxer. Violet lived with her mother, Lilian, who seems to have exerted a great deal of influence over Violet.

In the spring of 1934 while Reg was away in Jersey, Lilian discovered her young daughter was pregnant. She flew into a terrible rage. Immediately on his return she greeted Reg with the words, 'You have done the mischief – now you will have to stand for it.'

According to Reg he never had any intention other than to make an honest women of Vie although it is puzzling why the marriage did not take place until August 24th that year. The baby was born on October 14th.

Initially the young couple lived with Reg's parents at Hillside Farm but within a few weeks Reg had secured a job as cowman with Albert Cheeseman of Ivy House Farm, Oborne, Nr Sherborne and with it went a cottage.

Perhaps all would have been well if the young pair had been left to their own devices but unfortunately Lilian Smith seems to have been the archetypal mother-in-law. She egged Violet on to complain about the sparsity of the furnishings in her new home and to demand more housekeeping.

Perhaps in retaliation, Reg started to play the heavy-handed husband, laying down the law, especially with reference to her afternoon outings with the baby which, one imagines, usually took her back to her old home. In all probability she would return in nagging mode, fresh ideas having been fed into her by mother. This led to tears from Violet which meant her mother could sympathise and fan the flames of discontent.

Things came to a head in November when Lilian paid a visit and found her daughter in floods of tears. Reg informed her: 'I tell thee, she shan't go out today.' Violet cut in, 'Mother, I can't come up home of an afternoon or he says he will strangle me. If I sit on the sofa he swears I am half-canned.'

A few weeks earlier there had been an argument over Violet's wish to attend the Armistice Day service in town and this, no doubt, and other past grievances were raked up again. Reg left to go to work and Lilian began to urge Violet to get her things together. She had decided that her daughter and grandson were going home with her.

Reg returned home to an empty cottage with the fire gone out and no food on the table. He had to come to terms with the fact that Violet had gone. He was totally devastated. He stuck it out for a couple of days in the hope she would relent but eventually went back to his mother's. He pondered ways to persuade Vie to come back to him and enlisted the assistance of Albert Berriman, a lay reader at Sherborne Abbey, to write a pleading letter on his behalf. He promised he 'would give up boxing and do better by her'. The words fell on deaf ears.

Reg then consulted his boss, Albert Cheeseman and asked him if he could use his influence to cajole Vie into returning. The two of them went to Milborne Port and sat down and talked with Violet but she was adamant she would not return to the cottage and said she was considering going into service.

On Sunday December 9th, Reg met Vie's brother and after talking together for some time Reg decided to have another go at winning Vie back.

So what was in Reg Woolmington's mind when he cycled over to Milborne Port on that grey, breezy morning of December 10th, 1934? Was the sawn-off shot gun concealed beneath his coat to be used to frighten Violet, to end his life or to end her's? According to Reg's testimony – 'I thought out a plan to get her back. I thought if I threatened to take my life she would do so and the gun would show that I intended to kill myself. I sawed off the barrels to conceal it from my wife in case she had decided to come back to me.'

The plan had been formulated earlier that morning while he was milking the cows. When he had finished the task he took the gun to a barn and had sawn off the barrels. He then rode over to his mother's for breakfast.

It was soon after nine when Reg mounted his bike once more and

61

set out for Milborne Port. Violet was in the house, having just returned from her auntie's next door. When he arrived the auntie, Mrs Brine was pegging out washing in the garden and she heard him say 'Are you coming back or not?' followed by the query 'Where is your mother?' As Mrs Brine went back into her kitchen she heard a door slam at number 24 and then the sound of a shot rang out. She hurried to her front room window and saw Reg getting on his bike. She called out to him asking what he had done but either he did not hear her through the closed window or else he chose to ignore her.

Mrs Brine rushed into her sister's house and found Violet lying motionless on her side in the front room. The baby was in his pram nearby. There was no one else in the house – Lilian was away looking after her mother who was ill. Mrs Brine ran off to fetch help but it was too late to save Violet. The gunshot wound had been fatal.

Reg went straight to his mother's house and said 'I have shot Violet.' He then visited his boss, Albert Cheeseman announcing to him; 'I am not coming back to work anymore. I have been up and shot my wife.'

Sometime during that morning Reg's mother, Mrs Maria Woolmington found a note in one of her son's pockets. Several versions of this 'suicide' note were quoted by the press at that time so perhaps he had made several drafts. The note read:

Goodbye all. It is agonies to carry on any longer. I have kept true hoping she would return. This is the only way out. They ruined me and I will have my revenge. May God forgive me for doing this but it is the best thing. Her mother is no good on this earth. I have no more cartridges only two, one for her and one for me. I am of sound mind now. Forgive me for all the trouble caused. Goodbye all. I loved Violet with all my heart. Reg.

The trial of Reg Woolmington took place at Taunton in January 1935 when he was charged with wilful murder. Described as being of 'athletic build, dressed in a brown suit with handkerchief and tie to match,' he heard the judge, Mr Justice Finlay, order a re-trial as the jury could not agree on a verdict.

The re-trial took place in Bristol in February. It was while giving evidence here that Reg admitted writing the suicide note when he returned to his parents' farm after the shooting.

At 8.20 on the evening of St. Valentine's Day, 1935, the jury, after deliberating for one hour and thirty five minutes presented a verdict of 'Guilty' with 'a very strong recommendation to mercy.'

As things turned out, young Reginald Woolmington did escape the hangman's noose. He was lucky in being represented by a clever and determined counsel, Mr J.D. Casswell who submitted to the Court of Criminal Appeal the objection that the onus as quoted in 'Archbold's Criminal Pleading' was on the defendant to prove that the crime for which he had been found guilty was 'something less than the murder for which he is charged'.

The case went to the House of Lords, Woolmington won his reprieve and the law was amended so that the same problem would not arise again.

One is left with the impression that Reg was lucky to escape with his life. The jury obviously did not believe his story of the gun going off accidently or that he was only prevented from killing himself afterwards by his father's intervention. Was he really so confused when he arrived at his mother's that he forgot to mention it was an accident? Even so it is impossible not to feel some sympathy for a man whose mother-in-law seemed so determined to upset his life and prevent a reconciliation with his wife.

The Bank Bandits who Boarded a Bus

It was approaching noon on Monday March 13th, 1950 and the number 28 bus from Avonmouth to the centre of Bristol wended its way across the Downs, stopping at the White Tree where some passengers climbed aboard. As it turned the corner into North View the vehicle slowed and two men jumped on. They ran upstairs followed by conductor Dennis Pullen who asked for their fares. 'In a minute,' they replied.

Alarm bells began to ring in the vicinity and the driver, Jack Martin, alerted by shouts from the street brought the bus to a halt. The two fugitives leapt off the bus and made their escape through the normally quiet roads of Westbury Park hotly pursued by bank officials, local shopkeepers and other passers-by. Robert Taylor, a 30-year-old Fishponds man who worked for the *Evening World*

63

newspaper was fitter than most and was rapidly closing in on the fleeing pair when the stockier of the two turned, aimed a revolver, and shot Taylor at point blank range. His companion had already beaten off another would-be captor and the two took flight again as Taylor lay bleeding to death on the pavement. Although an ambulance arrived in double-quick time and rushed him to the Bristol Royal Infirmary, the brave Taylor died of his dreadful injuries.

Mr R.G. Taylor, the dead man.

In the meantime a local business man, James Ballinger, who ran a building company in nearby Etloe Road had called the police, realizing a bank raid had taken place at Lloyds on the corner of North View. The villains were soon apprehended as they fled in the direction of Redland Green.

The robbers were soon identified as Roman Redel and Zbigniew Gower, two young Poles who shared a room in a house in City Road, St. Pauls owned by the Wong family. It was Redel who fired the fatal shot. They were both 23 years old and had, until recently, worked as labourers. Gower was an orphan who had lost both parents in an air raid on Poland during the Second World War and had been forced to work for the Germans in Austria from 1943–45 when he had volunteered to join the Polish Corps. He had fought with the eigth army in Italy. Gower was demobbed in 1947 and had worked in England ever since. His last job had been with the British Oil and Cake Mills at Avonmouth where he had worked with Redel. They had both given up their jobs a week before the robbery.

The trial took place at Salisbury Assizes at the request of the defence, who obviously thought a local jury would be too heavily prejudiced against the young Poles. They were probably right as feelings locally ran high for the callous slaughter of the gallant Robert Taylor.

An account of the botched bank raid emerged at the trial. Gower, apparently, had suggested the plan on the day they had walked out of their jobs at B.O.C.M. On the Sunday they had carried out a 'recce' and decided on their escape route. As far as means of transport to aid their getaway – well, they hadn't really come up with any clear-cut ideas on that score although the idea of using a motor bike was mooted. Whether either of the young men possessed such a machine does not appear to have been established. Perhaps they intended to 'borrow' one?

The day of the proposed robbery dawned and Gower and Redel spent the early part of the morning in their lodgings finalizing the details. They had been confederates for three years, working together on various building sites before starting employment at the Cake Mills. Just why Roman Redel was sharing lodgings with Gower is unclear since a year previously he had moved out when he had married a 17-year-old blonde usherette who was also Polish. Anyway, be that as it may, this chill Monday morning found the two embryo gangsters embibing gin (they managed to put away a bottle between them before departing on their evil errand). Gower also topped up with a couple of bottles of beer so it is obvious their heads were not exactly crystal-clear.

They had sought to disguise themselves by wearing, in Redel's case, a pair of horn rimmed glasses and a cap, in Gower's, a beret and goggles. Thus equipped they set out for Westbury Park on a double-decker bus, Redel carrying in his pocket a six-chambered revolver and ammunition.

They reached Lloyds Bank, North View at a little after half past eleven. Mr Ronald Wall, the cashier, had just popped into the manager's office for a cup of tea leaving Mr John Bullock, the security guard, standing on the customers' side of the counter. Redel led the way into the bank, took out his gun and pointed it at Mr Bullock, instructing him to stay where he was. He explained, 'This is a hold-up.' He then indicated with his revolver the door to the manager's office and ordered Bullock inside. At this point Mr Wall emerged and he, too, was ordered back. Redel stood in the doorway covering the men with the gun while Gower climbed over the counter and proceeded to ransack the drawers. His haul was a mere £28 in notes plus some cheques and documents. The two desperadoes then backed out of the building, Redel still keeping the gun pointed at the bank staff. It was then the 28 bus appeared and they leapt aboard.

When their attempt to evade capture failed they took the course of action which was to result in the death of Robert Taylor. It was ironic Robert George Taylor who had fought for his country in North Africa, Italy and Sicily during the Second World War and survived should meet such an awful death five years later at the hands of two vicious young thugs when he was just going about his daily business.

Redel, in his defence, made the well-worn excuse 'The gun went off by accident,' adding that if he had been intent on killing he would have shot the bank staff, thereby ensuring his escape. Both men pleaded 'Not Guilty' to murder. Although they were permitted an interpreter both men had a reasonable command of the English language.

While the wheels of justice were being set in motion for the May trial of the two Poles, the guard at the bank, John Bullock, who lived in Falcondale Road, Westbury-on-Trym, received an unsigned threatening letter. It was written in ink in block capitals and bore a Bristol postmark. It was sent c/o Lloyds Bank, North View and read:

> You and Wall will get your deserts if our two boys hang. We are giving you fair warning so as to give you plenty of time to wish all your relatives goodbye.

Mr Bullock ignored the threat, handed the letter to the police and the trial went ahead.

Having heard all the evidence the jury only took one hour and ten minutes to reach a verdict of 'Guilty' although in Gower's case there was a strong recommendation to mercy. Of course had Redel been convicted of the lesser charge of manslaughter there would have been no case against Gower at all. Parallels were drawn with the famous de Antiquis case which had taken place in London a few years earlier. Alec de Antiquis, a married man with five young children, had attempted to foil some jewels thieves by blocking their path with his motor bike. He had been shot by one of the gang for his pains and although only one of the robbers was armed all were hanged for the murder.

Roman Redel's young wife was in court with a friend on the day that the sentence was pronounced. She had attended all the preliminary hearings and Redel had smiled at her from time to time from the dock. When the verdict was announced she broke down in tears and was comforted by a sympathetic policewoman.

The judge showed no mercy to Zbigniew Gower and both men

were executed at Winchester Gaol the following month, their appeals having been dismissed.

The whole tragedy of the case seems to rest on the total ineptitude of the young Poles, neither of whom had ever been in trouble with the law before. Did they honestly believe they would be able to calmly walk into the bank, commit the robbery and get away with the cash? Did they think their pathetic disguises would render them immune to recognition? Would they have acted so rashly had they not blurred their reasoning powers with over-ample amounts of alcohol?

The whole affair has all the elements of a farce had it not ended so tragically, leaving one with a feeling of immense sadness at the sheer waste of the life of handsome, athletic Robert Taylor. One wonders, too, how Roman Redel's blonde teenage bride coped with life afterwards as a murderer's widow.

Waylaid by a Wiltshire Wayside

How could one who rejoiced in the delightful nomeclature of Moses Angel be so inaptly named? He was certainly no angel and, far from being a law-maker, he was a law-breaker.

In 1827 Moses, the son of a Steeple Ashton butcher, was 19 years old. He was the second youngest of four boys and four girls. When he was not engaged in helping his father slaughter cattle he found casual farm work.

On November 20th, 1827 he encountered a pal of his, one George Winslow, who lived nearby and worked in Trowbridge as a gardener. George had left work at about five o'clock 'just as the lamps were being lit' and met up with Moses about three-quarters of a mile along the road. Moses was in conversation with a girl by the roadside. George called out 'Is that you, Moses? Are you going to Steeple Ashton?' Moses replied in the affirmative, left his companion and walked alongside George. When they reached Hilperton they decided to drop in at the 'Lion and Fiddle' for a glass or two of beer.

The Lion and Fiddle, Hilperton is said to be haunted. But is it the ghost of Daniel Bayley or Moses Angel? (Background information supplied by Jonathan Parker.)

The tavern was pretty full even at this comparatively early hour and there was a good deal of traffic between the bar and the kitchen, which served as a sort of extension to the bar. It was this constant movement between the two rooms which may account for the somewhat contradictory statements of witnesses later. Whether Richard Mizen was there all afternoon as the barmaid, Anna Pinnock, was later to testify or whether he left and then returned soon after the arrival of Moses Angel and George Winslow matters not. One thing that is certain is that just after Dr Daniel Bayley came in a few minutes before six o'clock, Mizen appeared in the bar and went into a huddle in the corner with Angel. Ten minutes later they both left and at the same time George Winslow noticed Daniel Bayley was gone. Winslow wandered over to the door. Was he looking for Moses or did he intend to continue to Steeple Ashton alone? In the event he met a friend of his called Giddings who was on his way in to the bar so Winslow retreated with him to the warmth of the interior. Twenty minutes later when they were contemplating going home Angel and Mizen reappeared in the bar.

Winslow and Giddings began their walk along the Steeple Ashton road and had only travelled about a hundred yards when they perceived a small crowd gathered by the roadside. They were clustered round the seemingly lifeless body of Daniel Bayley who was bleeding profusely from head wounds. A makeshift stretcher had been constructed on which to carry the injured man back to the inn. There he was made as comfortable as possible and a surgeon, Mr Mitchell, was called to dress his wounds.

At around noon on the following day, Bayley's daughter, Mrs Ann Pearce, came to collect him. She noticed that the silver watch and cash which had been on him when he left home were missing.

In spite of the care which was lavished on him by Ann and his wife, Jane, he became confused mentally and weak physically. Previously he had been a fit and healthy man aged 63. He died on December 15th as a result of his ordeal.

The day after the attack Moses Angel was to be found in the yard of the 'Wool Packs' at Trowbridge where he approached the ostler, Henry Pernall and asked if he wanted to buy a watch. At first Henry said 'No,' but Moses brought pressure to bear on him saying, 'I am broke down and I want some victuals and drink.'

Eventually Henry agreed and they both went into the pub for a beer. Henry observed Moses was in a somewhat dishevelled state with his 'small clothes torn'. He commented on this to Moses admonishing him with the words, 'it is not proper for a young man to have them so'. Moses explained that he had jumped over a hedge and a stake the previous night. On being asked by Henry how he had come by the watch he said that his father had just presented him with a four guinea one and he did not require two. Henry was obviously uneasy about the whole business and inquired as to how long he had owned the watch in question. 'Three years' was Moses' reply.

Later on Henry Pernall learned of Bayley's dreadful attack and went straight to Constable Foley with the timepiece, voicing his suspicions. Jane Bayley identified the watch as that which her husband had carried and Angel and Mizen were arrested on a charge of robbery. The charge of wilful murder was added later when Daniel died.

Richard Mizen was advised to make a deposition, in the form of a confession, by the tithingman who was acting as his gaoler. This was, however, judged inadmissable and not read out at the trial.

Moses Angel fell into a deep depression while in custody,

constantly crying and bewailing the fact that 'this is the fruits of keeping bad company. I would not be here if it was not for Mizen and Price.' Mizen was confined in an adjacent cell. He denied ever having spoken to Bayley before the fateful night.

John Angel came to visit his younger brother in prison. He berated Moses saying, 'If you had harkened to me it would not have happened'.

Moses argued that he would have gone straight home if it had not been for Mizen.

Moses' account of events was thus:

He said that when he entered the 'Lion and Fiddle' Mizen was already there with his friend Price. They took Moses outside and said Bayley was in the kitchen. They believed he had been to Trowbridge that day to collect his pension so they decided that when he left the inn they would follow him down the lane and rob him. To avert suspicion Mizen would alert Moses when Daniel Bayley left the pub by calling him James. They carried out their plan, Mizen removing his smock on the way and tossing it into a ditch. Moses alleged that Mizen then picked up a stone and crept up behind their victim, aiming at his head. Bayley fell to the ground begging 'Don't hurt me,' but Mizen ignored the plea picking up the stone with both hands and dashing it down on Bayley's head as he lay helpless on the track. They plundered his pockets and Moses took possession of the spoils, the silver watch, two half crowns and a sixpence. As they started to walk away Moses doubted that the man was dead and so returned and kicked him in the head. Later, in gaol, this fact seemed to disturb him most. 'I did kick him, I did,' he repeated, clasping his hands together in anguish at the memory.

He told how they left the insensible figure of Dr Bayley by the wayside and went in search of Mizen's smock. Having found this they made their way back to the tavern, Mizen, perhaps beginning to get cold feet about the whole affair, insisting Moses keep the watch. Each put half a crown into their pockets and the sixpence they spent on beer, saving some for the purchase of bread and cheese at a shop on their way home. All in all a small reward for the brutal death of an innocent man.

The jury, under the direction of Judge Littledale, swiftly reached a verdict – Moses Angel – Guilty of Wilful Murder; Richard Mizen – Not Guilty.

Before his execution at Fisherton Gaol in March 1828, Moses

Angel made a full confession to Rev. Hodgson believing he would 'meet with forgiveness for this and all the other sins in my life, through the all-atoning blood of my Redeemer.' He expressed regret for 'neglecting my church' and said he only once went to an alehouse on a Sunday. His reason for failing to attend religious ceremonies was that he had to stay home and look after his crippled mother. He admitted his parents used to 'advise me for my own good and warned me against going out poaching, to which I was very much inclined, but I did not heed to what they said. My father used to say it would bring me to some unhappy end. If I had listened to what they said I should not have been brought into the awful situation in which I now am.'

In the end one is left with a sneaky suspicion of sympathy for the young man taking his first step into the world of major crime with such disastrous results and left to face the music on his own. He tends to come across as a somewhat simple country boy getting out of his league with others who may have manipulated him. He certainly did not show any great intelligence in selling Bayley's watch the day after the robbery.

The Lion and Fiddle still stands in Hilperton dispensing ale, the present manager being Mr Justin Overingbury. Nearly two hundred years on, Moses Angel's infamy lives on as his shameful deed is recorded in old newspaper reports displayed on the pub walls. Incidentally the inn has a second claim to fame – that of being the only hostelry in the country which bears that name. Originally it was to be called 'The Cat and Fiddle' but the artist commissioned to paint the sign proved to be rather inept where animal representations were concerned. His cat looked exactly like a lion so, rather than go to the trouble of having the sign repainted, the pub was re-named.

Drink and Jealousy

It is likely that young Jane King, daughter of the landlord of the 'Rose and Crown' in Old Town Street, Plymouth, first met Henry John Honey, a musician, in her father's hostelry. If so, it was not an auspiscious omen for their future happiness, for throughout their turbulent three-year marriage his fondness for drink caused many problems.

Jane married him in 1832 when she was eighteen and he was a year older. The actual marriage was cloaked in secrecy and his parents were not told of the event until after the wedding. Mrs King who, after the death of Jane's father, took over the running of the pub paid all the wedding expenses so she was obviously in the young couple's confidence. A few months after the wedding Henry took off for America to find work, intending to send for his bride when he became established. But things did not pan out and within seven months he was back in Devon.

Even before this venture he had already been displaying signs of mental instability. On one occasion, just before his departure, he attempted to hang himself from a joist in his father's workshop and was saved only by chance when his mother came upon him and swiftly cut him down and revived him. When drunk he was insanely jealous where his wife was concerned although no suggestion is ever made by anyone that she gave him cause.

In the spring of 1834 Jane approached her mother-in-law Mary Honey, with whom she was on very affectionate terms, and begged that she and Henry be allowed to lodge in the family home at 14, King Street. She confessed she was terrified of Henry when he had been drinking because at such times he 'acted like a madman'.

It is obvious that he had a severe alcohol problem coupled with a personality disorder. During the time he and his wife lived with his parents Jane often had to ask her mother-in-law to take charge of knives, razors and a sword he kept in his room as she feared he would harm himself. When he was sober he professed to having no recollection of any of his drunken words or actions and at such times he generally behaved affectionately towards his wife and family

The Rose and Crown in Old Town Street, Plymouth, where Jane King probably met her future husband, Henry John Honey.

although he was known to sometimes deliberately destroy some of his mother's possessions, for no apparent reason.

Occasionally his behaviour warranted police intervention. He would then throw himself about in a frenzy and much of his fury seems to have been directed at his father, also a musician. Several times Henry Honey, Senior, was forced to quit the house. It would appear his mother exerted the stronger influence over him and was better able to calm him at such moments. More than once Jane was compelled to seek refuge in a neighbour's house to escape his illogical wrath.

In the early summer of 1835 Henry achieved a period of sobriety lasting five weeks. However on Monday June 29th, he received some money from an associate of his, a Mr Daniel of Cambridge Street and almost immediately went off the rails again. His excuse this time (for every bout drinker needs an excuse) was that rumours had been circulating regarding himself and a Mrs Smith of Cambridge Street, the wife of one of his cronies.

On the Friday of that week he arrived home for his tea at six o'clock 'very tipsy'. Jane upbraided him with the words 'If you go out again me and your mother will go out to walk,' to which he replied 'So you may.'

Directly after tea he went out again, not returning until midnight. Jane did not carry out her threat, remaining at home alone while

Mrs Honey went out. When Jane went down to breakfast the following morning, Saturday, she told her mother-in-law that Henry had come in late and had gone out that morning while she was still asleep. That afternoon a woman called at the Honey residence and informed Mary that her son was with a woman called Smith and 'his wife ought to know it'. Jane overheard the conversation and said she wanted to go out and look for him. She returned with her errant husband in tow at around 4.15 p.m. accusing him of being drunk and 'in a bad house'. She reproached him for not returning for his dinner.

While they were having tea Mrs King arrived brandishing an anonymous letter she had received regarding Henry's alleged liaison with Mrs Smith. She launched a diatribe at him until his mother intervened and attempted to defuse the situation. Henry decided to quit the house once more, his usual ploy it would seem when things were not going his way. He returned for supper and then it was off on the town again. He staggered in at eleven o'clock, so inebriated that Jane had to help him after he collapsed at the bottom of the stairs.

When Jane came down to breakfast on Sunday morning she gave the appearance of being quite happy although, once again, Henry was missing. He had left the house at half past six. Jane was going to her mother's for lunch and she started to get ready soon after ten o'clock. She was a pretty girl who enjoyed looking her best. She fastened on a coral necklace and donned a brown veiled bonnet, a gift from Henry. By eleven o'clock she was ready to depart. Elizabeth Coates, Henry's maternal grandmother who also lived at the King Street house, said she would accompany Jane part of the way as she was going in the same direction. Before the two women were half way down King Street Jane cried out 'There he is.' Henry was to be perceived approaching from the eastern end of the street. 'Never mind, go on,' urged Mrs Coates noticing that Jane was becoming extremely agitated. As Henry drew level he demanded 'Where do you think you're going?' His grandmother answered firmly 'She is going to her mother's and I am going to leave her there on my to the Lamb.'

Henry ignored his grandmother and said to Jane 'Turn back. I want you.' Seeing Jane was going to obey her husband's command, Mrs Coates thought she had better return to the house as well. After they had walked a few paces Jane commented, 'How dirty you are. Where have you been?' to which Henry replied 'I have been to

Bovisands – look at my hands.' He spread out his hands for her inspection and they certainly were blistered as though he had been rowing a boat. In fact his whole appearance was thoroughly unkempt, 'Very dirty and pale and weather-beaten as if he had been jaunting about,' as his mother was later to testify. Jane said she did not believe him but he ignored this and demanded to know if his clean clothes were ready. It seems he had made up his mind to accompany her to her mother's. As they neared the Honey residence Henry suddenly darted across the road and banged on the door of the 'Barley Sheaf' which was situated almost opposite their house. Jane dashed into the house saying to Mrs Coates that she would fetch his clean clothes downstairs but scarcely had she done this when her husband returned. She pointed out the clothes in the kitchen but he said 'I choose to go up.' Mrs Coates said to Jane 'He can't get in, can he?' and Jane answered 'Yes, he has the key.' After a couple of minutes he called out to Jane to come up. Jane confided to his mother 'He is mazed as a sheep,' and added she feared if she went up he would 'take off her bonnet and detain her at home'. Mrs Honey offered to go up with the clean clothes but Jane thought it better if she acceded to her husband's request. Mrs Honey warned her 'Don't scold if you do.'

Jane went upstairs and raised voices could be heard. Meanwhile Zach, Mrs King's porter arrived to find out what was causing the delay. Mary Honey went up to see when the young couple would be ready and Henry told her not to come in as he was not dressed. As she went down again to attend to a delivery of bread the argument in the bedroom continued.

Suddenly those waiting below in the kitchen heard the sound of running footsteps on the stairs. Mrs Honey was just quick enough to catch a glimpse of Jane fleeing through the front door crying 'I will go!' Henry then appeared on the stairs only partially dressed and enquired of his mother 'Where's Jane?' to which Mary replied sharply 'She has gone to her mother's to be sure. Why should you wish to stop her?' as Henry shouted out 'Good God – she has cut her throat!'

Mary ran out into the street and saw Jane standing by their neighbours' front door. She rushed over to her saying 'What have you done, dear Jane?' The girl collapsed in Mary's arms. Blood seeped through the fingers of her left hand which she held to her throat. Mary carried Jane into the passeway of number 14 and laid her at the foot of the stairs as she was unable to open the door through to the back parlour. She sent her servant Mary Warner to fetch medical assistance.

Dr Hingston soon appeared on the scene and managed to staunch the flow of blood but Jane became agitated and her convulsive movements caused the blood to spurt once more. 'Is there any hope?' she whispered. In her dying moments she kissed her mother-in-law and murmured 'Henry did it with a razor.'

Henry, meanwhile, was distraught. He swallowed the contents of a phial of laudanum which, combined with the alcohol he had consumed earlier caused him to fall into a deep sleep shortly after his arrest when he was taken to the Guildhall and placed in the Mayor's room. When he awoke in the early evening he was informed that his wife had died and he became hysterical. A Unitarian pastor was summoned who brought some comfort to the prisoner. Two guards remained with him throughout the night fearing he might make another attempt on his life.

When the case came to trial in August 1835 young Henry Honey, arrayed in a black suit and with a black silk handkerchief at his neck, gave a good account of himself. After the family had outlined the somewhat chequered existence of the couple and detailed the unfortunate Jane's last moments Henry's deposition was read out by an officer of the court.

The jury had already heard the evidence of William Sargent, landlord of the quaintly-named 'North Country Pink' on the Barbican. He told how Henry had called at the hostelry on the morning of Sunday June 5th and had partaken of a glass of purl and two glasses of brandy and water and had enquired as to the whereabouts of the nearest barber as he wanted to look tidy in order he could go to church. He confided in mine host that he was experiencing domestic problems owing to rumours which had been circulating about his relationships with other women. The landlord judged him to be sober and sedate at this stage.

Henry's testimony took the form of an emotional appeal to the jury. He asked them to ignore the lurid stories published by the press. He said 'If . . . for a moment you have believed that their history of this melancholy event is true, then I hardly hope that what I have to say will clear me in your eyes.' He trusted they would see 'I am not the great sinner I am supposed to be, nor guilty of the malicious murder of one whom I was bound to cherish and protect and for whom I always felt in my heart the strongest affection.'

He stated he had left home on that fateful morning soon after six and had returned between ten and eleven o'clock. Having been unable to locate a barber he had come home to shave himself. He then deposed that Jane brought up his clean clothes and they spent an hour together in their room during which time 'that connection passed between us that proven affection between husband and wife and not malice.'

He went on to explain that while he was shaving Jane raised the subject of his alleged infidelities and some sharp words were exchanged. She then insisted she had to leave to visit her mother. 'I asked her to wait for me,' said Henry. 'She would not, but insisted on going to her mother's before I was ready to go with her.' Then, according to Henry, she dodged behind him to get to the door and he seized her, forgetting the razor was in his hand. It was in this way the fatal injury to her throat was incurred.

The judge then gave a lengthy explanation of the difference between accidental death, manslaughter and wilful murder. It took the jury a mere five minutes to reach a verdict of 'Manslaughter' and Henry Honey was sentenced to transportation for life.

Although it is quite conceivable that Henry did not plan the murder of his wife and the fatal wound was administered accidentally in the struggle, his story of the loving hour the two of them spent together completely contradicts the statements of the other people present in the house. They all give the impression the quarrel began as soon as Jane entered the bedroom. Although if she and Grandma Coates left the house originally at eleven o'clock and met Henry almost at once and the actual death did not occur until after noon then the time element would rather favour Henry's version. Perhaps it was natural reticence that caused Mesdames Coates and Honey, snr., to gloss over these events.

Jane was buried on July 16th in the Burial Ground attached to the Ebenezer Wesleyan Chapel in Old Town Street. The funeral was arranged for six o'clock in the morning to avoid the prying eyes of sensation-seeking observers but when the sad little procession which included Jane's mother, brother and sister and Henry's parents left the 'Rose and Crown' they found the street lined with spectators nevertheless, as was the graveyard.

At the ceremony the choir sang 'Vital Spark' as the family wept for a squandered life.

Emily from 'The Early Dawn'

Emily Gardner was an attractive, high-spirited girl possessed of a superb figure. She was a great asset to her parents whom she helped in running 'The Early Dawn' public house in High Street, Cheltenham in 1871. She had a sister Alice to whom she was very close. Alice was in service at Saxham Villas, near Pittville, about a mile away.

Emily had an admirer, one Frederick Jones. Fred was a 21-year-old baker who lived with his parents in Swindon Place. He regarded Emily as the love of his life and, while she may have been flattered up to a point, she often found his devotion rather cloying and his jealousy irritating. As 1871 drew to a close he was becoming increasingly critical of her free and easy manner with the lodgers at her parents' inn. He also confronted her and Alice with a rumour which had come to his ears. Someone had said the girls had some 'unsuitable' books in their possession. Emily and Alice denied owning any such literature and announced that when they next encountered the false informant Alice would ask him if 'he meant what he said' and Emily would 'pitch into him'. The whole episode upset Fred abnormally and later he admitted that he swore to himself at that point he would kill Emily if he caught her speaking to another man.

It is clear that Emily had not the slightest notion of the depths of his passion. She continued to regale him with anecdotes about the lodgers, describing 'larkins and bits of fun with this chap and another'.

Perhaps she should have gained an inkling of the dark side of his nature when several times he made the suggestion that they 'go away together and destroy themselves'. This, he was to say later, was on occasions when he heard her mother 'going on about her and telling her she wished she was going to follow her to the grave.' What this was all about is never satisfactorily explained.

On Friday December 8th an incident took place which was to shape the future disastrous events. Fred came to the pub and on his way through the kitchen he saw Emily sitting with one of the lodgers.

She was apparently asleep (though he thought she could have been feigning) but what really upset him was the fact that Jack the lodger had his hand on Emily's knee. Fred admitted later 'It made me feel savage because I thought that showed there was something else between them.'

Later the same evening Emily was drawing some beer and one of the lodgers leaned over her shoulder to pull a pint for himself. This was witnessed by the lovelorn suitor and so inflamed him that he made a remark about this act of familiarity. He received a sharp riposte with reference to his excessive jealousy from the said lodger.

The situation was little improved by Sunday December 10th. Fred spent the afternoon at the Early Dawn but saw little of Emily as she spent all afternoon with the lodgers in their quarters in preference to sitting with Fred. He went home to tea and returned to the pub at about six o'clock still dwelling on the situation. Who knows what grim thoughts were churning in his mind as he removed Emily's father's razor from its customary place and secreted it in his pocket.

Emily and Alice decided to go for a walk and invited Fred to join them. Throughout the stroll on that dark December night he kept thinking about the razor and from time to time was tempted to throw it away but in the end he held on to it.

After the walk, they all made for home, the two girls returning to the pub and Fred back to Swindon Place for his supper. When he went back to the Early Dawn a little later Emily was putting on her outdoor clothes in readiness to accompany Alice back to her workplace. Fred was asked if he would care to escort them and, of course, he was only too delighted to say 'Yes'.

Fred and Emily bid goodbye to Alice at Saxham Villas and turned back the way they had come. It was very cold and Emily tucked her hands in her muff. The route they took was the one Emily always chose, and Fred had often asked her 'What makes you so fond of going that way?' which seems to indicate he suspected her of having some ulterior motive for following that particular path. His paranoia must have been extremely difficult for Emily to cope with at times.

As they walked by the light of the pale December moon Fred said to her, 'You seem to care for those humbugging lodgers more than you do for me, for you have been sitting in their company all evening.'

He then took her to task regarding the intimacy with Jack two nights previously. 'Don't bother me,' was her rejoinder, 'I shall do as I like.' He then asked, 'Do you care for me or no?' but she refused him an answer which so frustrated and infuriated him that he brought out the purloined weapon and shouted, 'I will make you tell me, or I will cut your throat, and with your own father's razor!'

Poor Emily was shocked and terrified and began to scream out 'Murder'.

'I will murder you if I am to hang for it the next minute,' he snarled putting his arm across her chest and pushing her against a wall. He began to slash her throat and face and, as they fell struggling to the ground, Fred received a razor cut to his face. As she lay in the roadway he dealt her the final fatal blow then dragged her body to a roadside ditch 'so that it should not be run over or that,' as he afterwards explained.

Although the scuffle was heard by several passers by it was thought merely to be a fight between drunken men and no one interfered. This was about ten o'clock.

By quarter to eleven Jones had reached his home and had told his father he had 'murdered Gardner's daughter'. Someone fetched Emily's father and Jones admitted killing her but swore it was in self-defence. It was Emily, he insisted, who had been in possession of the razor and she had threatened him with it and in the ensuing struggle Emily had died.

Jones stuck to this tale at his trial but after being found guilty he confessed the truth. He blamed his monstrous behaviour on the amount of alcohol he had consumed. He said he had loved her then and he still did and bitterly regretted what he had done. He hoped she was in heaven and no longer had any wish to live himself. He ended by saying, 'I do not seem to dread what is before me; and I pray every hour for the Lord to have mercy on me and forgive me. I can see it all now it is too late.'

Frederick Jones was executed in Gloucester Prison on January 8th, 1872, the first execution to be carried out since the abolition of public hangings. He was just one month short of his 21st birthday.